本书系 2024 年度河南省软科学研究计划

走进
中原民俗文化 （汉英对照）

TO UNDERSTAND THE
FOLKLORE CULTURE OF
THE CENTRAL PLAINS

孙 强◎主编

知识产权出版社

全国百佳图书出版单位

—北京—

图书在版编目（CIP）数据

走进中原民俗文化 = To Understand the Folklore Culture of the Central Plains.
汉英对照 / 孙强主编 . —北京：知识产权出版社，2025. 6. — ISBN 978–7–
5130–9719–2

Ⅰ . K892.461
中国国家版本馆 CIP 数据核字第 2024VT8003 号

内容简介

中原地区是中华文明的摇篮，中原文化是中华文化的重要源头和核心组成部分。本书将中原地区的民俗文化整理后分为物质民俗文化、社会民俗文化和精神民俗文化三个部分，并对之进行了详细的介绍，以帮助人们了解中华文明最重要的根系文化——中原民俗文化。

研究中原民俗文化，不仅是对传统文化的传承与保护，更是对民族精神的弘扬与发扬。深入了解这些宝贵文化遗产的内涵，有助于增强民族凝聚力，让更多中国人了解和认同自己的文化根源，从而增强民族自豪感和文化自信，同时促进中原民俗文化的传承、保护和对外交流。

责任编辑：徐家春　　　　　　　　　　**责任印制：孙婷婷**

执行编辑：赵蔚然

走进中原民俗文化
TO UNDERSTAND THE FOLKLORE CULTURE OF THE CENTRAL PLAINS
ZOUJIN ZHONGYUAN MINSU WENHUA
（汉英对照）

孙　强　主编

出版发行：知识产权出版社有限责任公司	网　址：http://www.ipph.cn		
电　话：010–82004826		http://www.laichushu.com	
社　址：北京市海淀区气象路50号院	邮　编：100081		
责编电话：010–82000860转8072	责编邮箱：823236309@qq.com		
发行电话：010–82000860转8101	发行传真：010–82000893		
印　刷：北京中献拓方科技发展有限公司	经　销：新华书店、各大网上书店及相关专业书店		
开　本：720mm×1000mm　1/16	印　张：12.75		
版　次：2025年6月第1版	印　次：2025年6月第1次印刷		
字　数：233千字	定　价：58.00元		
ISBN 978-7-5130-9719-2			

前　言

　　民俗文化是民族文化的基础，是民族精神的重要载体。保护、传承与发展民俗文化，就是在固守我们民族的根脉，就是在保护民族文化的DNA。中原民俗文化具有典型的根文化特征，对中国民俗文化乃至民族文化都有着重大的影响。但是，有关中原民俗文化的研究，特别是整体系统的研究很少，除了网络上介绍某种中原民俗文化，以中英双语的形式介绍和研究各种中原民俗文化的著作是没有的。因此，《走进中原民俗文化（汉英对照）》拟对各种典型的中原民俗文化进行较为全面的介绍，让人们系统了解中华文明最重要的根系文化——中原民俗文化。

　　本书是2024年度河南省软科学研究计划项目（编号为242400410338）的研究成果，并得到了河南理工大学科技处和外国语学院的支持，在此表示感谢。

　　在进行此研究的过程中，由于时间、人手有限，搜集资料的任务比较繁重，而且搜集资料的渠道也比较狭窄，所以没有将部分中原民俗文化罗列出来；罗列出的中原民俗文化资料也并不完全。在这种情况下，尽管研究者承担的压力比较大，但还是竭尽全力，付出一切时间和精力来完成此项研究。此项研究是研究中原民俗文化及其对外传播的一个开端，后期还会对此进行深度研究。

编　者

2025 年 6 月 10 日

Preface

Folklore culture is the foundation of national culture and an important carrier of national spirit. To protect, inherit and develop folklore culture is to stick to the root of our nation and to protect the DNA of national culture. Folklore Culture of the Central Plains has typical root cultural characteristics, and it has great influence on Chinese folklore culture and even Chinese national culture. However, there are few studies on the Central Plains folklore culture, especially comprehensive and systematic ones. In addition to introducing some kind of Central Plains folklore cultures on the Internet, there are no works introducing and studying various Central Plains folklore cultures in both Chinese and English. Therefore, *To Understand the Folklore Culture of the Central Plains (Chinese-English Edition)* intends to give a comprehensive introduction to various typical Folklore Culture of the Central Plains, so that people can systematically understand the most important root culture of Chinese civilization—Folklore Culture of the Central Plains.

This book is the research achievement of the 2024 Henan Province Soft Science Research Program with the project number 242400410338, supported by Office of Science and Technology and School of Foreign Studies of Henan Polytechnic University. I would like to express my gratitude to all of them.

Meanwhile, in the process of this research, due to the limited time and manpower, heavy task and narrow channels of collecting data, some kinds of Folklore Culture of the Central Plains are not listed possibly. In addition, the listed Central Plains folk culture data are not complete. In such a situation, although the researchers were under great pressure, they still did their best and devoted all their time and energy to completing this study. The research marks the beginning of the study on the folk culture of the Central Plains and its dissemination abroad, and in-depth research will be carried out on this topic in the future.

Author

June 10, 2025

目　录
Contents

上篇　物质民俗文化
Part I　Material Folklore Culture

中篇　社会民俗文化
Part II　Social Folklore Culture

Part III　Spiritual Folklore Culture
下篇　精神民俗文化

上篇　物质民俗文化

Part I　Material Folklore Culture

第一章 开封汴绣

汴绣是中国传统刺绣工艺之一，历史悠久，素有"国宝"之称。它以绣工精致、针法细密、图案严谨、格调高雅、色彩秀丽而著称，早在宋代就已驰名全国。2006年，汴绣被确定为河南省首批非物质文化遗产之一；2008年，汴绣被列入第二批国家级非物质文化遗产名录。

汴绣是一种历史悠久的绣种，多以人物风景为题材，其色彩搭配较其他绣种更为明快、奔放。底料用的都是织物密度很高的塔夫绸或者杭州缎，双面绣还要用透明的纱；用线全是蚕丝，并且不同的作品为了展现不同的效果和不同的工艺，通常会把一根丝线劈成若干丝。汴绣是纯手工制作而成，人为因素决定了每一幅作品都具有唯一性。

进入20世纪90年代，为了更好地适应时代的发展，汴绣在针法上进行了创新：双面绣、洒线绣、反戗绣、辫子股绣、盘金绣、盘银绣、席篾绣、打籽绣、编绣、发绣、滚针绣、垫绣，以及双面异色绣、双面三异绣等。

汴绣以绣制中国名画、古画著称于世，绣品古朴、典型、细腻。汴绣古画的代表作品有北宋画家张择端的《清明上河图》，五代南唐顾闳中的《韩熙载夜宴图》，唐代韩滉的《五牛图》、张萱的《虢国夫人游春图》、阎立本的《步辇图》，以及宋代武宗元的《朝元仙仗图》，宋代皇帝赵佶的《听琴图》，元代任仁发的《二马图》，清代意大利籍画家郎世宁的《百骏图》等。

　　汴绣，继承了宋绣的题材、工艺特点，借鉴了苏绣、湘绣等姊妹绣艺的长处，吸收了河南民间刺绣的乡土风味，并在此基础上创新了大量针法。其既长于花鸟虫鱼、飞禽走兽，又善于描绘山水图景，刻画人物形象细致传神。汴绣绣品既有苏绣雅洁活泼的风格，又有湘绣明快豪放的特点，从而形成了绣工精致细腻、色彩古朴典雅、层次分明、形象逼真的特色。

Chapter 1
Kaifeng Bian Embroidery

Bian Embroidery, one of the traditional Chinese embroidery techniques, has a long history and is known as "national treasure". It is famous for its exquisite embroidery, fine needlework, rigorous design, elegant style and beautiful color. It has been well-known throughout the country as early as the Song Dynasty. In 2006, Bian Embroidery was identified as one of the first batch of Intangible Cultural Heritage in Henan Province; in 2008, Bian Embroidery was included in the second batch of National Intangible Cultural Heritage List.

Bian Embroidery is a kind of embroidery with a long history, mostly themed around figures and landscapes. Its color collocation is more lively and unrestrained than other embroideries. The base material is taffeta or Hangzhou satin with high fabric density, transparent yarn is used for double-sided embroidery; all the yarn is silk, and in order to reflect different effects and different crafts for different works, a silk thread is usually split into several silks. Because Bian Embroidery is made by hand, human factors determine that each piece of work is unique.

In the 1990s, in order to better adapt to the development of the times, some novel embroidery methods were innovated: double-sided embroidery, thread-spraying embroidery, reverse embroidery, braid embroidery, coild gold embroidery, coiled silver embroidery, mat embroidery, seed stitch embroidery, knitting embroidery, hair embroidery, twisted stitch embroidery, padded embroidery, double-sided embroidery with varied colours, double-sided and three-distinction embroidery, and so on.

Bian Embroidery is famous for embroidering famous and ancient Chinese paintings, which is simple, typical and exquisite. Representative Bian Embroidery works include *Along the River During the Qingming Festival* by Zhang Zeduan in the Northern Song Dynasty; *the Night Revels of Han Xizai* by Gu Hongzhong in the Southern Tang of the Five Dynasties; *Five Oxen* by Han Huang, *the Painting of Lady of Guo on a Spring Outing* by Zhang Xuan, *Emperor Taizong Receiving the Tibetan Envoy* by Yan Liben in the Tang Dynasty; *Procession of Immortals Paying Homage to the Primordial* by Wu Zongyuan in the Song Dynasty; *Listening to Guqin* by Zhao Ji in the Song Dynasty; *Two Horses* by Ren Renfa in the Yuan Dynasty; *One Hundred Horses* by the Italian painter Lang Shining (Giuseppe Castiglione) of the Qing Dynasty and so on.

Bian Embroidery inherits the themes and technological characteristics of Song Embroidery, draws advantages of sister embroidery such as Su Embroidery and Hunan Embroidery, absorbs the local flavor of Henan folk embroidery, and innovates a lot of needling methods on this basis. Bian Embroidery is good at not only flowers, birds, insects, fish, beasts, but also landscape sceneries. They depict the characters meticulously and vividly. Bian Embroidery has both the elegant and lively style of Su Embroidery and the bright and bold features of Hunan Embroidery, thus forming the characteristics with exquisite and delicate, simple and elegant in color, distinct in level and vivid in image.

第二章　洛阳水席

　　洛阳水席，是河南省洛阳市一带的特色传统名宴，属于豫菜系。洛阳水席始于唐代，至今已有 1000 多年的历史，是中国迄今保留下来的历史最久远的名宴之一，俗称"千年盛宴"。2018 年，洛阳水席被评为"中国菜"之河南十大主题名宴。

　　水席起源于洛阳，这与其地理气候有直接关系。洛阳四面环山，雨少而干燥。古时洛阳天气寒冷，因此民间膳食多用酸辣的汤类，以抵御干燥寒冷。人们习惯使用当地出产的淀粉、莲菜、山药、萝卜、白菜等制作经济实惠、汤水丰盛的宴席，久而久之逐步创造出了极富地方特色的洛阳水席，并逐渐形成"酸辣味殊，清爽利口"的风味。

　　洛阳水席的"水"有两个含义：一是全部热菜皆有汤——汤汤水水；二是吃完一道，撤后再上一道，像流水一样不断地更新。

　　洛阳水席的特点是有荤有素、选料广泛、可简可繁、味道多样，酸、辣、甜、咸俱全，舒适可口。全席共设 24 道菜，包括 8 个冷盘、4 个大件、8 个中件、4 个压桌菜，冷热、荤素、甜咸、酸辣兼而有之。上菜顺序极为考究，先上 8 个冷盘作为下酒菜；待客人酒过三巡再上热菜：首先上 4 大件热菜，每上一道跟上 2 道中件（也叫陪衬菜或调味菜），美其名曰"带子上朝"；最后上 4 道压桌菜，其中有一道鸡蛋汤，又称送客汤，以示全席已经上满。

洛阳水席的好处在于一个"变"字，时代发展，南北交汇，水席食谱也在不断更新。纵然是三日一宴，也会发现新鲜可口的菜式，不至厌腻，而且凉菜热菜都是如此。

洛阳水席，历史悠久，古今驰名。红白大事，宴请宾客，率先用之。作为传统名宴，洛阳水席和牡丹花会、龙门石窟并称为"洛阳三绝"，被誉为古都洛阳的三大异风，成为洛阳人的骄傲。

Chapter 2
Luoyang Shui Xi

Luoyang Shui Xi is a traditional feast with characteristics in Luoyang, Henan Province, which belongs to the Henan Cuisine. Luoyang Shui Xi began in the Tang Dynasty, and has a history of more than 1000 years. It is one of the oldest famous banquets in China, commonly known as the "Millennium Banquet". Luoyang Shui Xi was awarded the top ten theme banquets in Henan Province of "Chinese cuisine" in 2018.

Shui Xi originated in Luoyang, which is directly related to its geographical climate. Luoyang is surrounded by mountains with little rain and dry weather. In ancient times, the weather was cold, therefore, folklore cuisines prefer to use sour and spicy soups to resist the dry and cold. People are accustomed to using starch, lotus, yam, radish, Chinese cabbage and other local products to produce economical and soupy banquets. Over time, Luoyang Shui Xi with rich local characteristics has gradually been created, and gradually formed a "hot and sour, refreshing and delicious" flavor.

There are two meanings of "Shui" of Luoyang Shui Xi: one is that all hot dishes have gravy—a lot of liquor; the other is that after eating one, the eaten-up plate will be retracted and next dish is updated as running water.

Luoyang Shui Xi is characterized by balance portion of vegetables and meat, wide selection of materials, being adjustable, diverse taste including sour, hot, sweet, salty, comforting and delicious. There are 24 dishes in Luoyang Shui Xi, including 8 cold dishes, 4 large dishes, 8 medium dishes and 4 table-pressing dishes, covering hot and cold, meat and vegetable, sweet and salty, sour and hot. The order of serving is very elegant, starting with 8 cold dishes to go with the liquor; waiting for guests to drink three rounds before serving hot dishes: 4 large hot dishes, each followed by two medium dishes (also known as accompanying dishes or condiments), called by a good name of "Take the Son to Court"; finally, 4 table-pressing dishes served, one of which is egg soup, also known as "Deliver Soup", to show that the whole table is full.

The benefits of the Luoyang Shui Xi lie in the word "change", with the development of the times and the intersection of north and south, generate the constant updating of the Shui Xi's recipes. Even if hold a Luoyang Shui Xi every three days, you will still find fresh and delicious dishes, not to be bored, it's the same regardless of hot or cold dishes.

Luoyang Shui Xi has a long history and is well-known in ancient and modern times. Whether wedding or funeral, it's inevitable that Luoyang Shui Xi will be the first to be used when entertaining guests. As a famous traditional banquet, Luoyang Shui Xi, Peony Flower Fair and Longmen Grottoes are known as the "Three Wonders of Luoyang", and are also known as the three unique customs of the ancient capital Luoyang, which has become the pride of Luoyang people.

第三章　开封夜市

从北宋开始，夜市就成为开封的一道亮丽风景并延续至今。每当夜幕降临，华灯初上，香味四溢的小吃车便充斥开封各主要街道，婉转悠扬的叫卖声夹杂着餐具的碰撞声不绝于耳，各种风味的小吃令人胃口大开，流连忘返。夜市是开封这座古城的一大特色。

周朝时，开封已经有日落后售卖饮食的摊贩，但尚未形成有规模的饮食夜市。唐中叶以后，长安（今西安）曾经出现过夜市，但很快被"宣令禁断"的诏令禁止了。到了北宋，开封成为宋王朝的都城，经济发达，百业兴盛，商业活动打破了坊与市的界限，处处店铺林立，饮食夜市不仅大量出现，而且非常繁荣。

开封夜市上的经营品种更是数不胜数，主要以小吃、特产、菜肴等开封美食为主，汤鲜鱼嫩的黄焖鱼、热鲜嫩香的炒凉粉、汤味醇厚的羊双肠、酥松适口的花生糕、清凉沙甜的冰糖梨枣、桶子鸡、五香风干兔肉等各色美食应有尽有。同时引进外地小吃，如新疆的羊肉串、北京的切糕、陕西的凉皮、广东的云吞等。

开封夜市自 1985 年以来，逐步由自发形成的小夜市发展成为政府正式批准的正规夜市。1995 年经开封市政府正式行文批准的夜市有 17 个。其中，开封鼓楼夜市有以广场为主的 3000 多平方米的饮食区，因其风味独特、传统小吃多而最为有名，在全国也屈指可数。

开封小吃源于夏商，盛于北宋，历经千年长盛不衰，在我国饮食文化历史上享有较高的地位。开封小吃有240多种，其中获得"中华名吃"称号的有70多种，获得"河南名吃"称号的有100多种。丰富独特的美食、悠久的历史奠定了开封夜市的地位。

Chapter 3
Kaifeng Night Market

Since the Northern Song Dynasty, the night market has become a beautiful scenery in Kaifeng, and continues to this day. When night falls and the lights are lit, the fragrant snack carts fill the main streets of Kaifeng. The euphemistic and melodious shouting is accompanied by the collision of tableware. The various flavors of snacks are appetizing and lingering. Night market is one of the characteristics of Kaifeng.

In Zhou Dynasty, there were vendors selling food after sunset, but there was no large-scale night market. Ever since the middle of Tang Dynasty, night markets appeared in Chang'an (now Xi'an), but they were soon banned by a decree "declaring a ban". In the Northern Song Dynasty, Kaifeng became the capital of the Song Dynasty, with a developed economy and prosperous industries. It broke the boundaries between residential district and markets, and there were shops everywhere. The night market for catering not only appeared in large numbers, but also was very prosperous.

There are countless varieties in Kaifeng Night Market. They are mainly snacks, specialties, dishes, and other Kaifeng delicacies. They include braised fish with fresh soup and tender fish, fried jelly with warm and tender taste, mutton sausages with mellow soup, crisp and delicious peanut cakes, cool and sweet pear dates with rock sugar, barrel chicken, and five-spiced dried rabbit meat. At the same time, non-local snacks such as mutton kebabs in Xinjiang, Qiegao in Beijing, Liangpi in Shaanxi and wonton in Guangdong were introduced.

Since 1985, Kaifeng Night Market has gradually developed from a spontaneous small night market to a formal night market approved by the government. There were 17 night markets approved by Kaifeng municipal government in 1995. Among them, Kaifeng Drum Tower Night Market has 3000 square meters catering area, is famous for its unique flavor and many traditional snacks, which is also one of the few in the country.

Kaifeng snacks originated from Xia Dynasty and Shang Dynasty, flourished in Northern Song Dynasty, have been famous for thousands of years. Kaifeng snacks enjoy a high status in the history of Chinese food culture. There are more than 240 kinds of Kaifeng snacks. Among them, more than 70 kinds have won the title of "Chinese Famous Delicacies", and more than 100 kinds have won the title of "Henan Famous Delicacies". Rich and unique delicacies and long history have established the status of Kaifeng Night Market.

第四章　道口烧鸡

　　道口烧鸡是我国特色传统名菜之一，由河南省滑县道口镇"义兴张"世家烧鸡店所制。道口烧鸡与符离集烧鸡、北京烤鸭、金华火腿齐名。道口烧鸡烧制时使用多种名贵中药，辅之陈年老汤，其成品色泽鲜艳、形如元宝、口衔瑞蚨，极具食疗和保健功能。1981 年被评为"全国名特优产品"。

　　道口烧鸡创始于清顺治十八年（1661 年），距今已有三百多年的历史，起初制作不得法，生意并不兴隆。乾隆五十二年（1787 年），"义兴张"的先祖张炳从清宫御膳房的御厨那里求得烧鸡制作秘方，做出的鸡十分香美。张炳的烧鸡技术历代相传，始终保持独特的风味，其色、香、味、烂被称为"四绝"。

　　清嘉庆年间，道口烧鸡成了清廷的贡品。张炳的子孙后代继承和发展了祖先的精湛技艺，使烧鸡一直保持着它的独特风味。20 世纪 70 年代以来，各国驻华使节和国外来宾吃了"道口烧鸡"，无不交口称赞。

　　道口烧鸡制作方法如下：准备一只新鲜的草鸡，剁去鸡爪，把两侧的肋骨割断；在草鸡的身上刷上一层蜂蜜水；锅里烧油，把草鸡放进锅里，中火炸至表面上色之后捞出；把陈皮、肉桂、豆蔻、丁香、白芷、砂仁、草果、生姜放在纱布中，做成调料包；锅里烧水，放入草鸡和料包，加上适量的盐、老抽、酱油，小火炖煮一个半小时；将煮好的烧鸡盛入盘子里，放凉即可食用。

道口烧鸡香味浓郁、酥香软烂、咸淡适口、肥而不腻，且新鲜出锅的烧鸡形如元宝，色泽金黄，尤为喜人。食用时不需要刀切，用手一抖，骨肉即可自行分离；无论凉热，食之均余香满口。

Chapter 4
Daokou Braised Chicken

Daokou Braised Chicken is one of the traditional specialties in China. It is made by Yixing Zhang family braised chicken shop in Daokou Town, Hua County, Henan Province. Daokou Braised Chicken is as famous as Fuliji Braised Chicken, Beijing Roast Duck and Jinhua Ham. With a variety of precious Chinese medicines, supplemented by the aged soup, the finished braised chicken is bright in color, shaped like a Yuanbao, with the auspicious coin in mouth. It has the functions of diet therapy and health care. In 1981, it was appraised as a "National Famous and Excellent Product".

Daokou Braised Chicken was created in the eighteenth year of Shunzhi reign in Qing Dynasty (1661) and has a history of more than three hundred years. At first, it was not made in the right way and its business was not prosperous. In the fifty-second year of Qianlong reign (1787), Zhang Bing, the ancestor of Yixing Zhang, sought the secret recipe of braised chicken from the imperial kitchen of the Imperial Kitchen of the Qing Palace, and made the chicken very fragrant and beautiful. Zhang Bing's braised chicken technology has been handed down from generation to generation, and has always maintained its unique flavor. Its color, fragrance, taste and softness are called "Four Excellences".

During the Jiaqing reign in the Qing Dynasty, Daokou Braised Chicken became a tribute of the Qing Dynasty. The descendants of Zhang Bing have inherited and developed the exquisite skills of their ancestors, so that the braised chicken has always maintained its unique flavor. Since the 1970s, all diplomatic envoys in China and foreign guests from all countries who have eaten "Daokou Braised Chicken", all spoken highly of it.

The preparation method of Daokou Braised Chicken is as follows: prepare a fresh grass chicken, cut off its claws and cut the ribs on both sides; brush a layer of honey water on the chicken's body; burn oil in the pot, fry the chicken in the pot until it is superficially colored, and then fish it out on the plate; put the dried orange peel, cinnamon, cardamom, cloves, angelica, amomum villosum, amomum tsaoko and ginger in the gauze cloth and make it into a seasoning packet; boil water in the pot and put grass chicken and seasoning packet into the water, add proper salt, light soy sauce, dark soy sauce, simmer for an hour and a half; put the cooked chicken in a plate, let it cool down and it's ready to be eaten.

Daokou Braised Chicken is rich in fragrance, crisp and tender, moderately salty, fat but not greasy. And the freshly cooked chicken is like a Yuanbao in shape and golden in color. Eating Daokou Braised Chicken does not require knife cutting, with a shake of the hand, the flesh and bones will be separated by themselves, whether hot or cold, the food is fragrant.

第五章　新郑大枣

新郑大枣指的是产地在河南省郑州市新郑的红枣，是新郑的特产，素有"灵宝苹果潼关梨，新郑大枣甜似蜜"的盛赞。

新郑种枣的历史最早可以追溯到8000多年前的裴李岗文化时期。春秋名相子产执政时，郑国都城内外街道两旁已是枣树成行。在汉代，人们已经认识到大枣的药用价值。到了明代，新郑枣树种植已形成相当规模。1949年以来，特别是改革开放以来，政府对发展大枣产业尤为重视，新郑大枣产业发展更趋区域化、规模化、科学化，新郑被命名为"中国红枣之乡"。

新郑大枣的早熟品种有六月鲜枣、奶头枣、八月炸枣（又名落花红）等。这些品种，皮薄肉脆、甜蜜多汁，宜鲜食。中熟品种有灰枣、鸡心枣、齐头白枣、铃枣、结不俗枣、新郑红枣、麦核枣、黑头羊枣、木枣等。

新郑大枣以其皮薄、肉厚、核小、味甜备受人们青睐，成为枣类中的佼佼者。它含有人体必需的18种氨基酸，内含蛋白质、脂肪、糖类、有机酸和磷、钙、铁及维生素B、维生素C、维生素P等物质，是天然的维生素果实，营养价值极高。常食大枣可缓解身体虚弱、神经衰弱、脾胃不和、消化不良、劳伤咳嗽、贫血消瘦等症状。

Chapter 5
Xinzheng Jujube

Xinzheng Jujube refers to the jujube originated in Xinzheng, Zhengzhou City, Henan Province. It is a special product of Xinzheng, and is known as "Lingbao apple Tongguan pear, Xinzheng Jujube sweet like honey".

The earliest history of jujube planting in Xinzheng can be traced back to the Peiligang culture period of more than 8000 years. When Zichan, the prime minister (in feudal China), was in power in the Spring and Autumn Period, the streets inside and outside the capital of Zheng State were lined with jujube trees. In the Han Dynasty, people had realized the medicinal value of jujube. By the Ming Dynasty, the cultivation of jujube trees in Xinzheng had formed a considerable scale. Since 1949, especially since the reform and opening-up, the government has paid special attention to the development of jujube industry, and the development of Xinzheng Jujube industry has become more regionalized, large-scale and scientific. Xinzheng has been named "the hometown of Chinese jujube".

The early-maturing varieties of Xinzheng Jujube include fresh jujube in June, nipple jujube, and mature jujube in August (also known as fallen flower red) and so on. These varieties have thin skin and crisp meat, and one sweet and juicy, suitable for fresh eating. Medium-maturing varieties are grey jujube, Jixin jujube, Qitoubai jujube, bell jujube, Jiebusu jujube, Xinzheng red jujube, wheat-kernel-shaped jujube, black-headed-sheep-shaped jujube and Mu jujube.

Xinzheng Jujube is favored by people for its thin skin, thick flesh, small nucleus and sweet taste, and has become the leader in jujube categories. It contains 18 essential amino-acids necessary for human body, as well as protein, fat, sugar, organic acid and phosphorus, calcium, iron, vitamin B, vitamin C, vitamin P and other substances. It is a natural vitamin fruit with high nutritional value. Eating jujubes regularly can relieve physical weakness, neurasthenia, spleen-stomach disharmony, dyspepsia, fatigue, cough, anemia and emaciation.

第六章　信阳茶叶

信阳是中国名茶之乡，具有2300多年的产茶历史。早在1200多年前，信阳便成为我国八大茶区之一。其中，信阳毛尖是"中国十大名茶"之一，也是河南省著名特产之一。茶是信阳的象征，也是信阳的传统特色优势产业。

民国初年，信阳茶区五大茶社产出的品质上乘的本山毛尖茶，被正式命名为"信阳毛尖"。信阳毛尖又称豫毛峰，属绿茶类，由汉族茶农创制。信阳市名茶产区分布在浉河区车云山、集云山、天云山、连云山、云雾山、黑龙潭、白龙潭、何家寨，俗称"五云两潭一寨"。

信阳毛尖色、香、味、形均有独特个性。其颜色鲜润、干净，不含杂质；香气高雅、清新；味道鲜爽、醇香、回甘；从外形上看匀整鲜绿有光泽，白毫明显。冲后香高持久，滋味浓醇，回甘生津，汤色明亮清澈。具有生津解渴、清心明目、提神醒脑、去腻消食等多种功效。

信阳毛尖被誉为"绿茶之王"。1915年，在巴拿马万国博览会上，信阳毛尖与贵州茅台同获金质奖；1990年，信阳毛尖品牌参加国家评比，获得绿茶综合品质第一名。

凭借"信阳毛尖"绿茶的品牌优势，自1992年起，"信阳茶文化节"便成为具有鲜明地方特色的民间节日。2010年，"信阳茶文化节"正式更名为"中国茶都·信阳国际茶文化节"。

Chapter 6
Xinyang Tea

Xinyang is the home of famous tea in China, has a tea-producing history of more than 2300 years. As early as more than 1200 years ago, Xinyang became one of the eight tea districts in China. Among them, Xinyang Maojian is one of the "Ten Famous Teas in China" and one of the famous specialties of Henan Province. Tea is the symbol of Xinyang, and also the traditional characteristic advantage industry of Xinyang.

In the early years of the Republic of China, high-quality Benshan Maojian Tea produced in the five tea houses in Xinyang Tea District was officially named "Xinyang Maojian". Xinyang Maojian, also known as Yumaofeng, is a kind of green tea, which was cultivated by Han tea farmers. The famous tea producing areas in Xinyang are distributed in Cheyun Mountain, Jiyun Mountain, Tianyun Mountain, Lianyun Mountain, Yunwu Mountain, Heilong pool, Bailong pool and He Jiazhai in Shihe District, commonly known as "Five Yun Mountains, Two Pools and One Village".

Xinyang Maojian has unique characteristics in its color, fragrance, taste and appearance. Its color is fresh, clean, free of impurities. Its fragrance is elegant and fresh. It tastes fresh, mellow, and leaves a pleasant sweet aftertaste. In terms of appearance, it is evenly shaped, bright green with a sheen, and the pekoe is clearly visible. After washing, the fragrance is high and lasting, the taste is rich and mellow, leaves a pleasant sweet aftertaste, promotes the secretion of saliva, and the tea water is bright and clear. It has many functions, such as producing saliva and slaking thirst, clearing heart and eyes, refreshing mind, removing greasiness and so on.

Xinyang Maojian is known as "the king of green tea". In 1915, Xinyang Maojian and Kweichow Moutai both won the Gold Medal at the Panama Pacific International Exposition. In 1990, Xinyang Maojian brand took part in the national evaluation and won the first place in the comprehensive quality of green tea.

"Xinyang Tea Culture Festival", relying on the brand advantage of "Xinyang Maojian" green tea, has become a folklore festival with distinctive local characteristics. In 2010, "Xinyang Tea Culture Festival" was officially renamed as "China Tea Capital—Xinyang International Tea Culture Festival".

第七章 灵宝苹果

灵宝苹果产于河南省灵宝市，色泽鲜艳、清甜爽口、营养丰富、耐贮耐运。灵宝市位于亚洲最佳苹果适生区和西北黄土高原优势苹果产业带的发源地。灵宝市苹果的栽培历史，清代县志已有记载。

灵宝地处河南、陕西和山西三省交界区域，秦岭以东，气候湿润，故而灵宝苹果拥有可以与山东苹果相媲美的品相，与新疆苹果相媲美的口感。灵宝苹果融东西地域的优点于一体，为中华苹果之翘楚，被誉为"中华名果"。灵宝栽培的苹果品种多达114种，主要品种有红富士、嘎啦、金冠、红星、华冠、秦冠、美八、乔纳金、国光等。

灵宝苹果色泽鲜艳红润、外表光滑细腻、口感浓香脆甜、蜡质层厚、含糖量高、抗氧化、耐储存，富含对人体有益的铁、锌、锰、钙等微量元素，经常食用，可帮助消化、养颜润肤。

Chapter 7
Lingbao Apple

Lingbao Apple is produced in Lingbao City, Henan Province. It has bright color, refreshing and sweet taste, rich nutrition, durable storage and transportation. It is located in the best apple growing area in Asia and the birthplace of the dominant apple industrial belt on the Loess Plateau in Northwest China. The cultivation history of Lingbao Apple is recorded in the county chronicles of the Qing Dynasty.

Lingbao is located in the junction area of Henan, Shaanxi and Shanxi provinces, east of Qinling Mountains, and the climate is humid, so Lingbao Apple has comparable appearance with Shandong Apple and the taste can be on a par with Xinjiang Apple. Lingbao Apple, which combines the advantages of eastern and western regions, is one of the best apples in China and is known as "the famous fruit of China". There are 114 Lingbao apple cultivars in Lingbao. The main cultivars are Red Fuji, Gala, Golden Crown, Red Star, Huaguan, Qinguan, Meiba, Jonagold and Guoguang, etc.

Lingbao Apple has bright red color, smooth and delicate appearance, fragrant crispy and sweet taste, thick wax layer, high sugar content, antioxidant, storage resistance, and is rich in trace elements such as iron, zinc, manganese, calcium and so on, that are beneficial to the human body. Eating it regularly can help with digestion and improve one's complexion as well as moisturize the skin.

第八章 武陟油茶

武陟油茶为河南省武陟县的特产，是国内素负盛名的风味小吃，至今已有 2600 多年历史。武陟油茶是一道色香味俱全的传统名点，秦朝称其为甘缪膏汤，汉朝称其为膏汤积壳茶，是我国历史悠久的传统特产、土贡食品。

早在两千多年前的秦朝末年，就有了武陟油茶的记载。相传楚汉相争时，刘邦受伤于武德县，住在一户昌姓人家中，昌氏为他做了膏汤积壳茶。膏汤积壳茶的味道令刘邦念念不忘，在他即位后，即封昌氏为五品油茶大师，封油茶为御膳。到清朝时，油茶仍流传于武陟。为治黄河水患，雍正皇帝曾亲临武陟监工，他在武陟品尝了当地著名的油茶，当即龙颜大展，这段佳话使吃油茶盛行起来。

武陟油茶名为茶，实际是粥。它的主料为精粉麦面，做粥之前，要先用油把面炒熟，所以人们称其为油茶。武陟油茶的原料除精粉麦面以外，还有淀粉、芝麻、花生、核桃仁、麻油等，另外还要加入茴香、花椒、肉桂、丁香、枇杷、砂仁、蔻仁等 24 种高级香料。

武陟油茶制作方法如下：首先，将面粉和淀粉混合，上笼蒸约 40 分钟。将芝麻过筛后炒成深黄色，碾碎；将花生用花生油炸焦，捞出晾凉去皮、压碎；将核桃仁碾成小粒。将面粉倒入锅中，用小火炒出香味，再分三次加入麻油，翻炒面粉至上色后，将花生、芝麻、核桃仁、盐、香料粉一起加入，继续炒拌几分钟后，油茶面即可出锅。炒好的油茶面要放在密封罐中，并在干燥处保存。食用时将油茶面取出，可冲食也可煮食。

武陟油茶色如咖啡，状如稀乳，吃起来香而不腻，咸甜适口，不仅味道浓郁，营养丰富，还有健胃提神的功能。

Chapter 8
Wuzhi Oil Tea

Wuzhi Oil Tea is a specialty of Wuzhi County, Henan Province. It is a famous snack in China with a history of more than 2600 years. Wuzhi Oil Tea is a famous traditional snack with excellent color, fragrance and flavor. In Qin Dynasty, it was called Ganliao Oil Soup, and in Han Dynasty, it was called the Gaotang Jike Tea, which is a traditional specialty with a long history in China, as the dedicated food.

As early as the end of the Qin Dynasty over two thousand years ago, there were records of Wuzhi Oil Tea. It is said that during the Chu-Han Contention, Liu Bang was wounded in Wude County and stayed at a household surnamed Lü. Lü made him Gaotang Jike Tea. The taste of Gaotang Jike Tea was so unforgettable to Liu Bang that after he ascended the throne, he conferred the title of Fifth-Rank Oil Tea Master upon the Lü and designated oil tea as a imperial food. Even in the Qing Dynasty, oil tea was still popular in Wuzhi. In order to control floods in the Yellow River, Emperor Yongzheng had personally visited Wuzhi to oversee the dams construction. He was extremely delighted as soon as he tasted the local famous oil tea in Wuzhi. This story makes eating oil tea became popular.

Wuzhi Oil Tea is called tea but is actually porridge. Its main ingredient is refined wheat flour. Before making porridge, the refined wheat flour should be fried with oil. So people call this porridge Oil Tea. In addition to refined wheat flour, the ingredients of Wuzhi Oil Tea include starch, sesame, peanut, walnut, sesame oil and so on. In addition, 24 kinds of high-grade spices such as fennel, Sichuan pepper, cinnamon, clove, loquat, amomum kernel and damom kernel are added.

The preparation methods are as follows: first, mix flour with starch, steam them in a cage for about 40 minutes. Stir-fry sesame seeds into deep yellow after sieving, and then crush; Fry peanut with peanut oil and scorched them out to cool, peel and crush; crush walnut kernels into small grains. Pour the flour into the pot, stir-fry over low heat until fragrant, add sesame oil in three separate batches, and stir-fry flour until colored, then add peanut, sesame, walnut, salt and spice powder together, and stir-fry for a few minutes before leaving the pot. The fried oil tea flour should be placed in an airtight jar and stored in a dry place. Take out when eating. It can be brewed and boiled.

The color of Wuzhi Oil Tea is like coffee, and the consistency is like thin milk. It tastes fragrant without being greasy, makes a pleasant balance of saltiness and sweetness. Wuzhi Oil Tea is not only rich in flavor and nutrition, but also has the function of strengthening stomach and refreshing.

第九章　叶县烩面

　　叶县烩面是一道美味可口的传统小吃，风味独特，堪称一绝。烩面采用优质面粉，细腻光滑，柔软筋香；烩面汤取新鲜的羊排、羊蹄骨，并放多味五香调料熬制而成，肥而不腻，淡而不薄，配上焦香辣椒油，色香味美。享誉周边十几个县市，属风味特色类小吃。

　　在 20 世纪 70 年代后期，叶县的杨文喜等几名匠心独运的厨师将炝锅面的做法和烩面的做法相结合，创造出了炝锅烩面。改革开放后，叶县炝锅烩面被推上市场化的道路，一带二，二传四，叶县烩面就做成了地方特色。

　　与主流的郑州烩面相比，炝锅是叶县烩面最与众不同之处。主流的郑州"萧记""合记"烩面做法是：煮好高汤，将烩面下进高汤里，盛出后，在汤面上点缀几片羊肉片；彼此不同仅在高汤的熬法。叶县烩面的特点则在于"炝"。它把鲜羊肉丝扔进锅里炒，嚓嚓声中，羊肉的味道彻底被炝了出来，再添加高汤，汤沸煮面。

　　叶县烩面特点是汤香肉美、鲜而不膻。而且，叶县烩面的拌料辣椒熟制过程工艺独特，至今仍秘而不宣。

Chapter 9
Ye County Stewed Noodle with Stir–Fried Sauce

Ye County Stewed Noodle with Stir-Fried Sauce is a delicious traditional snack, with unique flavor. Ye County Stewed Noolde with Stir-Fried Sauce using high-quality flour, which is delicate and smooth, with soft chewy taste; Ye County Stewed Noodle soup is made from fresh lamb chops and hoof bones, and is simmered with various five spice seasonings, it is rich but not greasy, light but not bland. Paired with the fragrant and spicy chili oil, it looks good, smells great and tastes delicious. It is well-known in more than a dozen counties and cities around Ye County and belongs to the category of flavor characteristics.

In the late 1970s, several ingenious chefs, such as Yang Wenxi, combined the method of Noodle in a stir-fried sauce with the method of stewed Noodle to create Stewed Noodle with Stir-Fried Sauce. After the reform and opening-up, the Stewed Noodle with Stir-Fried Sauce were put on the road of marketization. Spread through the market, the Stewed Noodle with Stir-Fried Sauce of Ye County became local characteristics.

Compared with the mainstream Zhengzhou stewed Noodle, Ye County Stewed Noodle with Stir-Fried Sauce are naturally different by stir-fried sauce.

Mainstream Zhengzhou "Xiao Ji" and "He Ji" practices are: cook the broth, put noodles into the soup, after being filled out, the soup surface is decorated with several pieces of mutton slices; the difference from mainstream Zhengzhou stewed noodle is only the boiling method of the soup. While the characteristics of Ye County Stewed Noodle with Stir-Fried Sauce is "stir-fried". It throws fresh mutton shreds into the pot and stir-fry, with the sound of rustling, the mutton taste was thoroughly stir-fried out, finally add soup and boil noodles.

Ye County Stewed Noodle with Stir-Fried Sauce is characterised by delicious soup and meat, fresh but not gamey. Moreover, the chili pepper, mixed with Ye County Stewed Noodle with Stir-Fried Sauce has a unique ripening process which is still secret.

第十章　开封灌汤包

开封灌汤包风味独特，已经有百年的历史，是开封著名美食之一。灌汤包皮薄，洁白如景德镇陶瓷，有透明之感；食之，内有肉馅，底层有鲜汤。开封人吃灌汤包有这样一句顺口溜："先开窗，后喝汤，一口吞，满口香。"灌汤包无疑是开封众多美食中璀璨的一颗星。

原来制作开封灌汤包的面是由三分之一的发面和三分之二的死面和成，后改为只用死面，不用发面，使其皮更薄，且不掉底。和面工艺要求颇严，要经过搓、甩、拉、拽，几次贴水、几次贴面的"三软三硬"的过程，才能达到要求。包子馅原掺有肉皮冻，吃多了腻口，后去掉了肉皮冻。又以白糖、味精调馅，去掉了甜酱，馅内只放姜末，不放葱。打馅则很费工夫，要一直把馅打得能扯长丝而不断。

开封灌汤包外形美观，小巧玲珑，皮薄馅多，灌汤流油，味道鲜美，清香利口，汤汁醇正浓郁，入口油而不腻。灌汤包皮薄洁白，包子上有精工捏制褶皱32道，均匀整齐；将其搁在白瓷盘上看，灌汤包似白菊；抬箸夹起来，悬如灯笼。

吃灌汤包，汤的存在列第一位，肉馅次之，面皮次次之。开封灌汤包随吃随蒸，就笼上桌；将吃面、吃肉、吃汤三者一体化，有一种整合的魅力。

Chapter 10
Kaifeng Guan Tang Bao

Kaifeng Guan Tang Bao has a unique flavor and has a history of 100 years. It is one of the famous foods in Kaifeng. The Guan Tang Bao has thin skin and the color is as white as Jingdezhen ceramics with transparent feeling. Eat it with meat filling and fresh soup on the bottom. Kaifeng people eat Guan Tang Bao with such a rhyme, "first open the window, then drink soup, next ingest it whole, finally full of fragrance". Guan Tang Bao is absolutely the most brilliant star in Kaifeng's many delicacies.

The original wrapper of Guan Tang Bao is made by one-third of the leavened dough and two-thirds of the unleavened dough, and then only the unleavened dough is used instead of the leavened dough, so that its wrapper is thinner and the bottom is not dropped. The technology of knead dough is quite strict. It can only be achieved by rubbing, flinging, pulling, pasting several times and "three softnesses and three hardnesses" of the process of adding water and flour. The filling was originally mixed with meat skin jelly. After eating too much, it was greasy and removed. Mix the stuffing with sugar and monosodium glutamate, removed the sweet sauce, filling with only ginger, not Chinese onions. It takes a lot of time to beat the stuffing, and the stuffing needs to be beaten until it can be stretched into long threads without breaking.

Kaifeng Guan Tang Bao has beautiful appearance, which is small and exquisite, thin and stuffed, filling soup with oil, and also has delicious taste, delicate fragrance and is pleasant to the palate, soup is pure and mellow, which tastes oily but not greasy. The wrapper is thin skin and white. There are 32 folds with fine kneading craft on the Guan Tang Bao, which is extremely uniform. Put it on a white porcelain plate, it looks like white chrysanthemum. Clip it up, hanging like lanterns.

When eating Guan Tang Bao, the presence of soup ranked first, followed by meat filling, the last is wrapper. Kaifeng Guan Tang Bao is steamed as you order and served in small steamer. Eating Guan Tang Bao becomes a integration of wrapper, meat and soup, is a kind of integrated charm.

第十一章 鲁山揽锅菜

揽锅菜是鲁山古老与现代精湛烹调技术相结合、精工细作的"杂烩菜",是河南省的传统名菜之一,属于豫菜。鲁山揽锅菜是鲁山这个山区小县唯一获得"河南名吃"称号的地方风味名菜,它因味美色鲜、质优价廉而深受人们的喜爱,不仅遍布鲁山城乡,而且跨县越省,全国不少地方都挂有"鲁山揽锅菜"的招牌。

据传,鲁山揽锅菜起源于明朝洪武年间,后经几代人的潜心研究,结合当地人酷爱咸鲜、滑嫩、香软的特点制作而成。这种菜品既受普通百姓喜爱,又具有地方特色。

鲁山揽锅菜配料考究,且营养价值颇高。主料是丸子、豆腐、粉条、蕨菜及时令蔬菜。豆腐是油焖过的;粉条精选本地上乘好粉,软软绵绵,内筋外熟;丸子由剔骨猪肉拌红薯淀粉,并经油炸而成;蕨菜是地道的山货;还有青的蒜薹、黄的金针菇、白的白菜、红的蕃菜。揽锅菜的调料选的是四川郫县豆瓣酱、广东老抽酱油和上等的四川花椒、胡椒,还有白芷、肉桂、陈皮、砂仁等数十种中草药配制的特等香料,形成风味独特的美味大餐。

"揽锅菜"的名称与"杂烩菜"相比,既传承了古老传统,又丰富了文化内涵。鲁山揽锅菜从选料、切片到烹调,流程科学合理,原料营养丰富,色彩斑斓,精工细作,工序考究。食后易于机体消化吸收,并且兼顾了中原人的饮食习惯，香而不腻，麻辣适度，既过瘾又解馋。鲁山揽锅菜主副兼备，荤素搭配，营养均衡。合理的烹调方法保证了营养成分，使菜肴色香味俱佳。鲁山揽锅菜配套主食为碗蒸的正宗原阳大米，香甜烂熟，还配有热腾腾的糯米酒米汤，香喷喷、甜滋滋，着实惹人喜爱。

Chapter 11
Lushan Casserole

Lushan Casserole is a kind of exquisitely crafted "miscellaneous dish" which combines ancient and modern cooking techniques in Lushan. It is one of the traditional famous dishes in Henan Province and belongs to the Henan Cuisine. Lushan Casserole is the only famous local dish in that mountainous county called Lushan, which has won the title of "Henan Famous Food". It is loved by people for its delicious taste, high quality and low price. It is not only popular in urban and rural areas of Lushan, but also across counties and provinces. There are signs of "Lushan Casserole" hanging in many parts of the country.

According to legend, it originated in Hongwu period of Ming Dynasty, and has been researched over generations, which made by combining with the local people's love for saltiness, tenderness, fragrance and softness. This kind of casserole is not only popular with ordinary people, but also has local characteristics.

The ingredients of Lushan Casserole are exquisite, and their nutritional value is quite high. The main ingredients are meatball, tofu, vermicelli, fern and seasonal vegetables. Tofu is braised in oil; vermicelli is made by the best local flour, soft, chewy inside and cooked outside; the meatball is made by pork and sweet potato starch fried; fern is an authentic mountain product; of course, there are green garlic moss, yellow needle mushroom, white Chinese cabbage, red Fancai. The seasonings of Lushan Casserole are Sichuan Pixian Douban Sauce, Guangdong dark soy sauce, Sichuan zanthoxylum bungeanum and pepper, as well as dozens kinds of premium-grade spices prepared from Chinese herbal medicines such as Angelica dahurica, cinnamon, dried orange peel and Amomum villosum, which form a delicious meal with unique flavor.

Comparing with the name of "miscellaneous dishes", the name of "Lushan Casserole" not only inherits the ancient tradition, but also enriches the cultural connotation. From ingredient selection, slicing to cooking, the process of Lushan Casserole is scientifically and reasonably and the raw materials are rich in nutrients, this dishes is colorful, elaborate and exquisite. Lushan Casserole is easy to digest and absorb after eating, and takes into account the dietary habits of the Central Plains people, fragrant but not greasy, moderately spicy, both addictive and satisfying. Lushan Casserole is a dish that combines main ingredients and side dishes, integrates meat and vegetables, and offers a balanced nutrition. Reasonable cooking method ensures the nutritional ingredients, with good color, aroma and taste. The staple food of Lushan Casserole is authentic Yuanyang rice steamed in a bowl. It is sweet and ripe. Lushan Casserole is also equipped with hot rice soup mixed with glutinous rice wine. It is delicious, sweet and truly loved by people.

第十二章 汝窑瓷器

汝窑是宋朝五大名窑之一，因位于汝州而得名，窑址在今河南省宝丰县大营镇清凉寺村。汝窑居宋代"汝、官、哥、钧、定"五大名窑之首，在中国陶瓷史上素有"汝窑为魁"之称。汝瓷是中华传统制瓷著名代表之一，也是中国北宋时期主要代表瓷器之一。目前，汝瓷是汝州市的一张代表名片。

汝瓷兴盛于北宋，因其专为宫廷烧制御用瓷器，亦称"汝官瓷"。汝瓷制作工艺精湛，用料考究，配方独特，烧瓷技艺高超，由于铁还原达到了最佳效果，超越了当时所有的窑口，是中国青瓷发展史上划时代的创举。北宋末年，汝窑烧瓷技法由于战乱而失传。元朝以来，历代仿烧不断，均难成功，所以留存于世的汝窑瓷器弥足珍贵，成为稀世珍宝。宋、元、明、清以来，宫廷汝瓷用器，皆为内库所藏，视若珍宝，与商彝周鼎比贵。

汝窑传承者以传承艺术为己任，采用传统手工制作陶瓷方法。制作一个陶瓷的工序多达十三道，包括淘泥、摞泥、拉坯、印坯、修坯、捺水、画坯、上釉、烧窑、成瓷、成瓷缺陷的修补等。做工精细，设计唯美。承艺汝瓷以"釉色层"领先，器形古朴，典雅得当，光润有度，手感润滑如脂。由于汝瓷釉层厚，常有开片如鱼鳞、蝉翼状，久用之后茶色会附着于裂纹处，形成不规则的变换交错的花纹，有似玉非玉之美。

　　汝瓷造型古朴大方，以名贵玛瑙为釉，色泽独特，有"玛瑙为釉古相传"的赞誉。随光变幻，观其釉色，犹如"雨过天晴云破处""千峰碧波翠色来"之美妙，坯体土质细润，其釉厚而声如磬，明亮而不刺目。器表呈蝉翼纹细小开片，有"梨皮、蟹爪、芝麻花"之特点，被世人称为"似玉非玉而胜玉"。

Chapter 12
Ru Kiln Porcelain

Ru Kiln, one of the five famous kilns in the Song Dynasty, is named for its place of origin "Ruzhou". The Ru Kiln is located in Qingliangsi Village, Daying Town, Baofeng County, Henan Province. Ru Kiln is the first of the five famous kilns in the Song Dynasty: Ru, Guan, Ge, Jun and Ding. It is known as "Ru Kiln is the top of kilns" in the history of Chinese ceramics. Ru Porcelain is one of the well-known traditional Chinese ceramic representatives, which is also one of the mainly represented porcelains in the Northern Song Dynasty. At present, Ru Porcelain is a representative card of Ruzhou City.

Ru Porcelain flourished in the Northern Song Dynasty, which was specially fired for the imperial court, also known as "Ru Official Porcelain". Ru Porcelain has exquisite craftsmanship, meticulous materials, unique formula and superb firing skills. Because of the best effect of iron reduction, it surpassed all kilns at that time and was an epoch-making innovation in the history of development of Chinese celadon. At the end of the Northern Song Dynasty, Ru Kiln firing techniques were lost because of the war. Since the Yuan Dynasty, numerous imitations have been made, but none have succeeded, so preserved Ru Porcelain is precious and becomes a rare treasure. Since the Song, Yuan, Ming and Qing Dynasties, the imperial porcelain from Ru Kiln had been treasured in the Inner

Palace Storehouse, which is as valuable as the bronze wares of Shang and Zhou Dynasties.

Inheritors of Ru Kiln take inheritance of art as their duty, adopt traditional handmade method to make ceramics. The ceramic-making process involves as many as 13 steps, including washing China Clay, laying China Clay, drawing greenware, printing greenware, repairing greenware, rubbing water, painting greenware, glazing, firing in kiln, forming ceramics, repairing defects of ceramics and so on. It has fine workmanship and beautiful design. Chengyi Ru Porcelain takes the lead in "glazing color layer". Its style is simple and elegant, with a proper luster and a smooth hand feel like grease. Because of the thick glaze layer of Ru Porcelain, there are often cracks like fish scales and cicada wings. After long use, the tea stain will adhere to the cracks, forming irregular and alternating patterns, presenting a beauty that is like jade but not exactly jade.

Ru Porcelain is simple and generous in shape, with precious agate as its glaze, resulting in a unique color. It has the praise of "agate as glaze handed down from ancient times". With the change of light, the glaze color is like "the clouds break down the sky after raining" "the green waves of thousands of peaks coming into view". The clay of the porcelain body is fine and smooth. Its glaze is thick, bright yet not glaring, and when tapped, it makes a sound like chime. The surface of the porcelain shows fine cracks like cicada wings, with the characteristics of "pear skin, crab claw, sesame flower" and is praised by the world as "resembling jade, not being jade, yet surpassing jade".

第十三章　宁陵张弓酒

　　张弓酒是河南省宁陵县特产，也是中国国家地理标志产品。它始于商，兴于汉，具有悠久的历史渊源和丰富的文化内涵。张弓酒具有"窖香浓郁、优雅细腻、绵甜爽净、醇厚丰满、回味悠长"的风格特点。2007年张弓酒被批准实施地理标志产品保护。2011年张弓酒被评为"中华老字号"。

　　张弓酿酒历史久远，从宁陵丁堌堆遗址、黄岗寺遗址发掘出的陶片、酒器可以看出，张弓酿酒的历史在4000年以上。至明清时期，张弓酿酒业已很兴盛。

　　宁陵县属黄淮流域，淮河水系；四季分明，气候温和；地下水资源丰富；土质为微酸黏性土壤，适合高粱、小麦、大麦、豌豆等酿酒用农作物的种植；环境良好，生态自然。千百年来的积淀，使这里形成了一个适宜各类酿酒微生物生长、繁殖的微生物群系，决定了张弓酒独特的品质。

　　张弓酒选用当地盛产的优质小麦、高粱为料；以高温曲、中温曲为糖化发酵剂；用纯净古泉井水加浆，固态发酵，老五甑混合蒸烧；以花生饼、菜叶、苹果、大曲粉等为原料培养窖泥；缓气蒸馏，低温入池，缓慢发酵，量质摘酒，分级入库，延长贮期，精心勾兑，成为成品；最后还要通过冷冻和活性炭吸附来过滤。长期适量饮用张弓酒，有理气活血、润喉爽神、增进健康之功效。其酒体丰满，窖香浓郁，清澈透明，甘爽凛冽，尾净味长，醇和适口。

Chapter 13
Ningling Zhanggong Liquor

Zhanggong Liquor, a local specialty of Ningling County, Henan Province, is a product with Geographic Indication of China. Zhanggong liquor originated in Shang Dynasty and flourished in Han Dynasty. It has a long history and rich cultural connotation. Zhanggong Liquor is characterized by its "strong cellar aroma, elegance and delicacy, sweetness and cleanliness, mellowness and richness, and long aftertaste". In 2007, Zhanggong Liquor was approved to be protected as a product with geographical indication. In 2011, it was awarded the title of "China Time-Honored Brand".

Zhanggong has a long history of liquor brewing. From the pottery tablets and liquor vessels excavated at Dinggudui site and Huanggang Temple site in Ningling, we can learn that Zhanggong's history of liquor brewing is over 4000 years. By the Ming and Qing Dynasties, Zhanggong's liquor brewing industry had flourished.

Ningling County belongs to the Huanghuai River Basin, the Huai River System. It has distinct seasons, mild climate, abundant groundwater resources and slightly acidic clayey soil, which is suitable for the cultivation of sorghum, wheat, barley, pea and other brewing crops. The environment is good and the ecology is natural. With thousands of years of accumulation, this area has formed a microbial community that is suitable for the growth and reproduction of various liquor-making microorganisms, determines the unique quality of Zhanggong liquor.

Zhanggong Liquor selects high-quality wheat and sorghum as raw materials; using high-temperature Daqu and medium-temperature Daqu as saccharifying starter, using pure Guquan well water as pulping, with solid-state fermentation, mixed steaming in old five steamers; cultivating pit mud with peanut cake, vegetable leaves, apple and Daqu powder; slow-gas distillation, low-temperature fermentation, slow-fermentation, quality liquor picking, grading into storage, appropriately prolonging storage period, meticulously blending and becoming mature product; and finally it has to be filtered by freezing and activated carbon adsorption. Long-term appropriate drinking Zhanggong Liquor can regulate Qi and invigorate the circulation of blood, moisten throat and refresh spirit, and improve health. Its liquor is full-bodied; cellar aroma is full-flavored; it's clear and transparent, sweet and refreshing, with no strange odors and its aroma lingers for a long time, and is mild and pleasant to the taste.

第十四章　宝丰酒

宝丰酒是中国名酒之一，以优质高粱为原料，大麦、小麦、豌豆混合制曲，陶瓷地缸发酵，采用"清蒸二次清"的酿造工艺，经续渣操作、水泥池地窖发酵、甑桶蒸馏、量质摘酒、长贮陈酿、精心勾兑等工序而酿成。宝丰酒具有清香纯正、甘润爽口、回味悠长等特点，是我国清香型白酒的典型代表之一。

宝丰酒史，源远流长。据史志记载，中国酿酒鼻祖之一的仪狄在宝丰造酒，距今已有4100多年。从古应国出土的古代酒器，也证明了宝丰酒悠久的历史。隋唐时，宝丰酒业得到了长足发展，唐朝还把宝丰酒定为贡酒，通过当时的东都洛阳送到长安。北宋时，宝丰酒业繁荣昌盛惊动朝廷，为规范酒业发展，朝廷官方设立"酒务"。当时汝州有十酒务，宝丰就有商酒务、封家庄、父城、曹村、守稠桑、宋村等七酒务。酒务是宋朝官方专门经营酒的地方，年收税万贯以上。宋神宗还钦派大理学家程颢监酒宝丰。金时，宝丰酒业兴盛不衰，资产万贯以上的作坊100余家，贩粮售酒者如流，监酒官有镇国上将军、忠校尉、忠显昭信尉等16人。

在河南三百多家酒企之中，称得上"中国名酒"的仅有两家，宝丰酒稳坐其中一席。而根据惯例以地名、人名、艺名三种命名法则来看，宝丰酒又是中国名酒中不多见的以地域命名的酒品。酒以地名，地因酒美。

在相当长的一段时期，宝丰酒与另外两个白酒品牌张弓酒和林河酒一道被世人并称"张、宝、林",这是约定俗成的名酒代名词,甚至早于时下的"茅、五、剑"。历史名人的推崇,既是宝丰酒久盛不衰的主要原因之一,如唐代著名诗人刘希夷(汝州人)就曾作诗赞美宝丰酒;也不断扩大了宝丰酒的知名度。知名度的扩大,既吸引更多的知名人士喜爱宝丰酒,又促进宝丰酒生产规模的不断发展和产品质量的稳定提高。

Chapter 14
Baofeng Liquor

Baofeng Liquor, one of China's famous liquors, is made from high-quality sorghum as raw material, mixing barley, wheat and pea to make Daqu, fermented in ceramic vat, using the brewing process of "steaming and clearing twice", through mixed distilland order way, fermentation in cement cellar, distillation in a still, quality-based liquor selection, long-term storage and aging, careful blending and other processes. Baofeng Liquor is a typical representative of Light Aroma Baijiu in China, which has the characteristics of pure fragrance, pleasant taste and long aftertaste.

Baofeng Liquor has a long history. According to historical records, Yidi, one of the originators of Chinese liquor-making, made liquor in Baofeng, it has a history of over more than 4100 years. From the ancient liquor vessels unearthed in Guyingguo, it is enough to prove that Baofeng Liquor has a long history. During the Sui and Tang Dynasties, Baofeng Liquor industry developed rapidly. In the Tang Dynasty, Baofeng Liquor was also designated as a tribute liquor, which was sent to Chang'an through Luoyang, the eastern capital at that time. In the Northern Song Dynasty, the prosperity of Baofeng Liquor industry shocked the court, the court officially established Liquor Bureau of the Song Dynsaty in order to standardize the development of the liquor industry. There were ten

Liquor Bureaus in Ruzhou and seven Liquor Bureaus in Baofeng, including Shangjiuwu, Fengjiazhuang, Father Town, Cao Village, Shouchousang and Song Village. Liquor Bureau is the official place of the Song Dynasty specializing in liquor, which collects more than ten thousand taxes annually. Cheng Hao, the great philosopher, was dispatched to supervise liquor-making in Baofeng by Emperor Shenzong of Song Dynasty. In Jin Dynasty, Baofeng Liquor industry was flourishing. There were more than 100 workshops with more than 10, 000 assets of Baofeng Liquor industry. Food and alcohol vendors were as much as flowing water. There were 16 liquor inspectors included senior general of Zhenguo, Zhong Xiaowei, Zhongxian Zhaoxin Wei and other officers.

Among the more than 300 liquor enterprises in Henan Province, only two of them are "Well-Known in China", among which Baofeng Liquor has a steady seat. According to the three nomenclature rules of place name, person name and art name, Baofeng Liquor is one of the most rare regional nomenclature liquors in China. Liquor is named by place and the place is well-known by liquor.

For quite a long time, Baofeng Liquor, together with the other two liquors Zhanggong Liquor and Linhe Liquor, were called "Zhang, Bao and Lin". This is a well-known liquor pronoun by convention, even earlier than the current "Mao, Wu and Jian". The esteem of historical celebrities, is not only one of the main reasons for Baofeng Liquor's lasting prosperity. For example, Liu Xiyi, a famous poet of the Tang Dynasty (Ruzhou person), wrote poems to praise Baofeng Liquor. But also it has continuously expanded the popularity of Baofeng Liquor. The increasing popularity not only attracts more famous people to like Baofeng Liquor, but also promotes the continuous development of Baofeng Liquor production scale and the stable improvement of product quality.

第十五章 焦作怀山药

焦作古称怀庆府，北依太行、南临黄河，自然条件得天独厚，怀山药、怀地黄、怀菊花、怀牛膝，这"四大怀药"驰名中外。怀山药作为"四大怀药"之首，医家评价其"温补""性平"，是"药食同源"的典范。

焦作市位于太行山与黄河之间的狭长冲积平原，土壤有着丰饶的矿物质元素，加之迎风坡、海拔、光热、水文等因素，栽种山药的历史悠久。

怀山药又名薯蓣，一名山芋，其根可药用，因其药效可与人参相比，又称"怀参"。为多年生缠绕性草本，根肉质肥厚，略呈柱形，长短不等。铁棍山药为怀山药中的珍品，因其色褐间红、质坚粉足、身细体长，外形酷似铁棍而得名，主产区为温县。铁棍山药按地理位置的不同分为临近黄河的沙土和垆土两种。铁棍山药根茎呈圆柱形，长 60～80 厘米，最长可达 100 厘米以上，身细而坚，水分少，汁液较浓，味道鲜美，入口"面而甜"，并伴有淡淡的麻味。

怀山药主要成分为皂苷、黏液质、胆碱、山药碱、淀粉、糖蛋白、自由氨基酸、多酚氧化酶、维生素 C、碘质、16 种氨基酸，以及铁、铜、锌、锰、钙等多种微量元素，具有健脾、补肺、固肾、宜脑、益智、养颜、抗衰老、抗疲劳、抗有害物质刺激、调节代谢、增强免疫机能、促进生长、调节内分泌、调节肾功能和神经系统的功能，是药用价值最高、滋补作用最佳的药食同源珍贵药材。经常食用，不但可以增强体质、滋养皮肤、延缓衰老，而且对腰痛、痛经、肾虚、食欲不振、食少便溏、脾虚泄泻、肺虚久咳、肥胖等颇有良效。

Chapter 15
Jiaozuo Huai Yam

Jiaozuo was historically known as Huaiqing Prefecture, Taihang Mountains in the north and Yellow River in the south. Its natural conditions are unique. The "Four Major Huai Medicines", namely Huai Yam, Huai Rehmannia Glutinosa, Huai Chrysanthemum and Huai Achyranthes Bidentata are famous at home and abroad. As the top of the "Four Major Huai Medicines", Huai Yam has been evaluated by doctors as having "warming and tonifying" properties and a "neutral nature", serving as a model of "food and medicine share the same origin".

Jiaozuo City is located in the long and narrow alluvial plain between the Taihang Mountains and the Yellow River. The soil here is rich in mineral elements. Coupled with windward slope, altitude, light, heat, hydrology and other factors, it has a long history of planting yams.

Huai Yam, also known as rhizoma dioscoreae or sweet potato. Its roots can be used for medicinal purposes. Because of its pharmacodynamics can be compared with ginseng, it is also known as "Huaishen". It is a perennial entangled herb with thick flesh and slightly columnar roots of varying lengths. The Iron Stick Yam is a treasure of Huai Yam. It is named for its brown-red color, firm and starchy texture, slender and long body, and its shape resembles an iron stick. The main producing area is Wen County. The Iron Stick Yam can be divided into two types according to its geographical location: sandy soil near the Yellow River and dark loessial soil. The Iron Stick Yam's rhizome is cylindrical, 60 to 80 centimeters long, and can even reach more than 100 centimeters in length. It's thin and firm, with less water, thick juice, a delicious taste, a "flourg and sweet" texture, and a faint numbness.

The main components of Huai Yam are saponins, mucus, choline, yam alkaloids, starch, glycoprotein, free amino acids, polyphenol oxidase, vitamin C, iodine, 16 kinds of amino acids, as well as iron, copper, zinc, manganese, calcium and other trace elements. It has many kinds of functions, such as invigorating the spleen, tonifying the lung, reinforcing the kidney, nourishing the brain, enhancing intelligence, nourishing the face, anti-aging, anti-fatigue, anti-harmful substance stimulation, regulating the metabolism, enhancing immune function, promoting growth, regulating endocrine, regulating renal function and nervous system function, has the highest medicinal value, the best nourishing effect of medicinal and food homologous precious medicinal materials. Eating frequently not only can strengthen the body, nourish the skin and delay aging, but also has a good effect on backache, dysmenorrhea, kidney deficiency, poor appetite, eating less and having loose stools, spleen deficiency diarrhea, lung deficiency, chronic cough, obesity and so on.

中篇　社会民俗文化

Part II　Social Folklore Culture

第一章　春节

　　春节是中国四大传统节日之一，中原俗称春节为"过年"或"大年"。春节是除旧布新的日子，虽定在农历正月初一，但春节的活动却并不止于正月初一这一天。春节不仅集中体现了中华民族的思想信仰、理想愿望、生活娱乐和文化心理，还是祈福、饮食和娱乐活动的狂欢式展示。

　　春节是中国民间最隆重盛大的传统节日，其起源历史悠久，由上古时代岁首祈年祭祀演变而来，在传承发展中承载了丰厚的历史文化底蕴。新春贺岁以祭祝祈年为中心，以除旧布新、迎禧接福、拜神祭祖、祈求丰年等活动展开，内容丰富多彩，热闹喜庆，年味浓郁，凝聚着中华文明的传统文化精华。

　　过了腊月初八，就开始准备年货。腊月二十三，俗称"小年"，祭灶王爷；腊月二十四扫尘（年终大扫除）；腊月二十五磨豆腐；腊月二十六买块肉；腊月二十七杀只鸡；腊月二十八贴春联；腊月二十九蒸馒头；腊月三十包饺子。除夕是农历腊月最后一天（有时没有腊月三十），从东汉开始，河南人把除夕惯称"大年三十儿"，民间最重要的活动是除夕之夜的祭祖和守岁。

　　正月初一，首先燃放鞭炮，拜祝先祖遗像。接着，晚辈向长辈拜年，长辈要给晚辈"压岁钱"。全家人吃过年饺子，随后开始到亲友家拜年。拜年是春节期间的一项重要活动，一直延续到正月十五元宵节。正月初二是出嫁的女儿回娘家的日子。正月初三为祭坟、祭祖宗的日子。初五为破五节，民间认为初五是年后第一个不吉日，亲友之间亦忌相互串访。

春节在传承发展中已形成了一些固定的习俗，如办年货、扫尘、贴年红、团年饭、守岁、发压岁钱、拜年、舞龙舞狮、拜神祭祖、烧爆竹、烧烟花、祈福、逛庙会、敲锣鼓、上灯酒、赏花灯等。传统的节日仪式与相关习俗活动，是节日元素的重要内容，承载着丰富多彩的节日文化内涵。

Chapter 1
Spring Festival

Spring Festival, one of the four major traditional festivals in China, is commonly known as the "Guonian" or "Danian" in the Central Plains. The Spring Festival is a time for getting rid of the old and welcome the new. Although the Spring Festival is set on the first day of the first lunar month, the activities of the Spring Festival are not limited to the first day of the first lunar month. The Spring Festival not only embodies the Chinese nation's thoughts and beliefs, ideals and aspirations, life and entertainment, culture and psychology, but also is a carnival display of blessings, feastings and entertainment activities.

Spring Festival is the grandest traditional festival among Chinese folklore. It has a long history. It evolved from praying and worshipping at the beginning of each year in ancient times. It bears a rich historical and cultural heritage in the inheritance and development. Celebrating Spring Festival is centered on the festival of offering sacrifices and praying for a good year, with the activities of getting rid of the old and welcoming the new, welcoming happiness and receiving blessings, worshipping gods and ancestors, and praying for a bumper harvest. The content is rich and colorful, lively and festive, with a strong flavor of the New Year, condensing the traditional cultural essence of Chinese civilization.

After the eighth day of the twelfth month of the lunar year, people begin to prepare the New Year's Goods. On the twenty-third day of the twelfth lunar month, commonly known as "Little New Year", people offer sacrifices to the Kitchen God. On the twenty-fourth day of the twelfth lunar month, people do the sweeping of dust (the year-end general cleaning). On the twenty-fifth day of the twelfth lunar month, people grind tofu. On the twenty-sixth day of the twelfth lunar month, people buy meat. On the twenty-seventh day of the twelfth lunar month, people kill a chicken. On the twenty-eighth day of the twelfth lunar month, people paste Spring Festival couplets. On the twenty-ninth day of the twelfth lunar month, people make steamed buns. On the thirtieth day of the twelfth lunar month, people make dumplings. New Year's Eve is the last day of the twelfth lunar month (sometimes there is no thirtieth day). Since the Eastern Han Dynasty, people in Henan have customarily called New Year's Eve "Danian Sanshier". The most important folk activities on New Year's Eve are offering sacrifices to ancestors and staying up late to welcome the New Year.

On the first day of the first lunar month, firecrackers are first set off to worship the portraits of ancestors. Then, the younger generation pays New Year's greetings to their elders, and the elders will give them "lucky money". The whole family eats dumplings for the Spring Festival and then begins to pay New Year's greetings to relatives and friends. New Year greeting is an important activity during the Spring Festival, which lasts until the Lantern Festival on the fifteenth day of the first lunar month. The second day of the first lunar month is the day when the married daughters visit their parents' home. The third day of the first lunar month is the date of offering sacrifices to graves and ancestors. The fifth day of the first lunar month is the "Po Wu" Festival. People believe that the fifth day of the first lunar month is the first unlucky day after the New

Year, and friends and relatives should not visit each other.

The Spring Festival has formed some fixed customs in its inheritance and development, such as preparing New Year's Goods, cleaning dust, pasting Spring Festival couplets and other decorations, having the reunion dinner, staying up late to welcome the New Year, giving out lucky money, paying New Year's greetings, performing dragon and lion dances, worshipping gods and ancestors, firing firecrackers, lighting fireworks, praying for blessings, visiting Miaohui (temple fairs), playing gongs and drums, holding lantern-lighting banquet, and enjoying the lanterns. Traditional festival ceremonies and related custom activities are important contents of festival elements, carrying rich and colorful festival cultural connotations.

第二章　元宵节

元宵节为每年的农历正月十五，素有"小过年""大十五"之说。元宵节又称上元节、小正月或灯节，是中国春节年俗中最后一个重要节令。正月是农历的元月，古人称"夜"为"宵"，所以把一年中第一个月圆之夜"正月十五"称为"元宵节"。中原元宵节民间活动内容丰富、规模盛大。2008 年 6 月，元宵节被列入第二批国家级非物质文化遗产。

元宵节民俗的形成有一个较长的过程，据一般的资料与民俗传说，正月十五在西汉已经受到重视，汉武帝正月上辛夜在甘泉宫祭祀"太一"的活动，被后人视作正月十五祭祀天神的先声。不过，正月十五元宵节真正作为民俗节日是在汉魏之后。正月十五燃灯的习俗与佛教东传有关。唐朝时，佛教大兴，仕官百姓普遍在正月十五这一天"燃灯供佛"。从唐代起，元宵张灯即成为法定之事，并逐渐成为民间习俗。

元宵节习俗自古以来就以热烈喜庆的观灯为主。除观灯外还有吃元宵、赏月、放烟花、猜灯谜、耍狮子、踩高跷、划旱船、扭秧歌、打太平鼓等传统民俗活动。"汤圆"与"团圆"字音相近，象征着团团圆圆、和睦相处。中原地区最独特的习俗，就是在元宵之夜，家家户户都得在祖宗墓前，用竹篾和红纸扎上灯笼，点燃其间的蜡烛任其燃尽。

元宵节主要活动是大众娱乐，但是其社会文化意义却不仅仅是娱乐，它承载着传承千年的民俗文化和民族情感。

Chapter 2
The Lantern Festival

The Lantern Festival, the fifteenth day of the first lunar month, is known as the "mini New Year's celebration" and "big fifteenth". The Lantern Festival, also known as the Shangyuan Festival, Xiaozhengyue or the Lamp Festival, is the last important festival in the Chinese Spring Festival customs. Zhengyue is the first month of the lunar calendar. The ancients called "night" as "Xiao", so the fifteenth day of the first lunar month in a year which is the first full moon night of the year, is called the Lantern Festival. The Lantern Festival activities among the folklore in the Central Plains are rich in content and grand in scale. In June 2008, the Lantern Festival was selected as the second batch of National Intangible Cultural Heritage.

The formation of the Lantern Festival folklore custom has a long process. According to general information and folklore, the fifteenth day of the first lunar month had received attention in the Western Han Dynasty. Emperor Wu's activities of offering sacrifices to the "Taiyi" in Ganquan Palace on the Shangxin night of the first lunar month were regarded as the forerunner of offering sacrifices to the gods on the fifteenth day of the first lunar month. However, the Lantern Festival on the fifteenth day of the first lunar month was regarded as a folk festival after the Han and Wei Dynasties. The custom of lighting lamps on the fifteenth day of the first lunar month is related to the spread of Buddhism.

In the Tang Dynasty, Buddhism was flourishing. Officials and ordinary people generally lighted lamps for Buddhism on the fifteenth day of the first lunar month. Since the Tang Dynasty, displaying lanterns have become a legal matter, and gradually become a folk custom.

The customs of Lantern Festival have mainly centered around the lively and festive activity of watching lanterns since ancient times. There are also traditional folk activities such as eating Tangyuan, enjoying the moon, setting off fireworks, guessing lantern riddles, performing lion dance, walking on stilts, rowing land boats, dancing Yangko and playing Taiping Drum. The pronunciation of "Tangyuan" is similar to that of "reunion" in Chinese, which symbolizes reunion and harmonious coexistence. The most unique custom in Central Plains is that on the night of the Lantern Festival, every family must tie lanterns with bamboo strips and red papers in front of their ancestors' tombs and light candles to burn them up.

The main activity of Lantern Festival is mass entertainment, but its social and cultural significance is not just entertainment, it carries the folk culture and national emotions that have been passed down for thousands of years.

第三章　龙抬头节

龙抬头（农历二月初二）又称春耕节、农事节、青龙节、春龙节等，是中国民间传统节日。"龙"是指二十八星宿中的东方青龙七宿星象，每到仲春卯月之初，"龙角星"就从东方地平线上升起，故称"龙抬头"。自古以来，人们在仲春"龙抬头"这天敬龙庆贺，以祈消灾赐福、风调雨顺、五谷丰登。

龙抬头是中国古代农耕文化在节令中的反映，其源于对自然天象的崇拜，与上古时期中国古人对星辰运行的认识和农业节气有关。中原地区长期为小农经济生产方式，历来崇拜能呼风唤雨的龙神。农历二月初二，正处在"雨水""惊蛰"和"春分"之间，民间认为，这天是龙欲升天的日子，故称"龙抬头节"或"青龙节"。这一天要开展各种各样的活动，一来祈求龙王降雨，二来祈福消灾祛毒。龙抬头这天，河南农村的妇女一般都不动剪刀，不做针线活，怕动了刀剪伤龙体。按老年人的说法，这是为了表示对龙的尊敬。在这个节日里，人们到田野里采野菜、包饺子、煎煎饼、炒黄豆、煎腊肉、蒸枣馍，改善生活成为节日的一项重要内容。"龙抬头"虽有着久远的历史源头，但它出现在文献上并与节俗联系在一起是在元代以后。元朝时开始把"二月二"称为"龙抬头"。

"龙抬头"是中国古代农耕文化对于节令的反映，标示着阳气自地底而出，春雷乍动、雨水增多、气温回升，万物生机盎然，春耕由此开始。自古以来龙抬头时节就是一个祈福纳祥转运的日子。

Chapter 3
The Dragon Head–Raising Day

The Dragon Head-Raising Day (the second day of the second lunar month), also known as the Spring Plowing Day, the Agricultural Day, the Green Dragon Festival, the Spring Dragon Festival and so on, is a traditional Chinese folk festival. "Dragon" in Chinese refers to the seven-star signs of the Oriental Green Dragon (Qinglong in Chinese) among the Twenty-Eight Constellations. Every time at the beginning of lunar February, "Dragon Horn Star" rises from the eastern horizon, so it is called "Dragon Head-Raising". Since ancient times, people have celebrated the day of "Dragon Head-Raising" in lunar February, in order to pray to eliminate disasters, bestow blessings, bring favorable weather for crops, and ensure a bumper harvest.

The Dragon Head-Raising is a reflection of the ancient farming culture of China in solar terms. Its origin is the worship of natural celestial phenomena, which is related to the understanding of stars' movement in ancient times and agricultural solar terms. The Central Plains region had been dominated by the small-scale peasant economy production mode for a long time and has always worshipped the Dragon who could summon wind and rain. The second day of the second lunar month falls between "Rain Water (Yushui in Chinese) ", " Waking of Insects (Jingzhe in Chinese)" and "Spring Equinox (Chunfen in Chinese)".

The folklore believes that this day is the day when the Dragon is about to ascend to the sky, so it is called the "Dragon Head-Raising Day" or "Green Dragon Festival". On this day, various activities will be carried out. Firstly, people will pray to the Dragon King for rain, and secondly, they will pray for blessings, to eliminate disasters and expel toxins. On that day, women in rural areas of Henan generally do not use scissors or do needlework, for they are afraid that using scissors would harm the Dragon's body. According to the elderly, this is to show respect for the Dragon. During this festival, people go to the fields to pick wild vegetables, make dumplings, fry pancakes, stir-fry soybeans, fry cured meat, steam date buns, improving living conditions has become an important part of the festival. Although "Dragon Head-Raising Day" has a long historical origin, it was after the Yuan Dynasty that it was mentioned in the literature and associated with festival customs. It was in the Yuan Dynasty that the "second day of the second lunar month" began to be called "Dragon Head-Raising Day".

"Dragon Head-Raising" is the reflection of ancient Chinese farming culture in solar terms. It indicates that Yang Qi comes out from the ground. Spring thunder rumbles, rainfall increases, temperature rises, all things are full of vitality. Spring farming begins from this day. Since ancient times, "Dragon Head-Raising Day" is a day to pray for blessings, receiving good fortune, and having a change of luck.

第四章　太昊陵庙会

　　太昊陵庙会是一种古老的传统民俗及民间宗教文化活动。太昊伏羲陵始建于春秋，汉代曾在陵前建祠，其规模之宏大、建筑之雄伟，世人叹绝。太昊陵庙会的声势之大、会期之长也为中原地区庙会所独有。太昊陵庙会每年自农历二月二日始，至农历三月三日止，会期一个月。它寄托了中国劳动人民祛邪、避灾、祈福的美好愿望。

　　太昊陵庙会的起源可以追溯到 6000 多年前，据史书记载，中华民族人文始祖太昊伏羲氏曾定都宛丘（今淮阳区）。在以此为中心的黄淮平原上，拉开了华夏文明的序幕。伏羲因此成为一个划时代的人物，被后世推崇为"三皇之首""人文始祖"，成为中华民族尊崇敬重的人祖、龙祖、中华共祖。为纪念伏羲的功德，在太昊伏羲氏的长眠之地淮阳建有陵庙。宋太祖赵匡胤诏立陵庙，自此始有固定的供祭之日。至明清两代又多次修葺扩建。太昊陵规模宏大、华彩璀璨、伟美壮观，使朝祖庙会更加红火、热闹非凡。

　　庙会期间各种各样的传统民俗娱乐活动更是引人入胜。其中以杂耍、表演最多，舞狮、龙灯、竹马、旱船等应有尽有。与其他庙会相比，太昊陵庙会习俗中有两个十分独特的地方。一是有"担经挑"，也称"担花篮"的比较原始的祭祖悦神的舞蹈。二是庙会上有随处可见的"泥泥狗"，这是庙会上出售的一种泥玩具，吹之有声。据考证，这些泥玩具是从原始社会后期流传至今的活文物。太昊陵庙会的民俗活动带有许多原始文化的色彩。

　　如今的太昊陵庙会，规模更加宏大，朝圣者已遍及全国各地。不少国际学者、友人也都在此期间来此寻古探幽，研究古老华夏的东方文明；港澳台同胞以及侨居国外的华夏子孙，每年都组团来太昊陵寻根问祖，并以到伏羲陵前谒祖朝拜为荣，以示不忘祖先、不忘自己是龙的传人。

Chapter 4
Taihaoling Temple Fair

Taihaoling Temple Fair is an ancient traditional folk custom and folk religious and cultural activity. Taihao Fuxi Mausoleum was built in the Spring and Autumn Period. In the Han Dynasty, ancestral halls were built in front of the mausoleum. The grand scale and magnificent architecture of the mausoleum made the people marvel at it. The scale of Taihaoling Temple Fair is so large and its duration is so long that it is unique among the temple fairs in the Central Plains region. The Taihaoling Temple Fair starts on the second day of the second lunar month and ends on the third day of the third lunar month every year, lasting for one month. It embodies the beautiful wishes of the Chinese working people to exorcise evil spirits, avoid disasters and pray for blessings.

The origin of Taihaoling Temple Fair can be traced back to more than 6000 years ago. According to historical records, the ancestor of the Chinese nation's humanities, Taihao Fuxi, once established the capital of Wanqiu (Today's Huaiyang County). On the Huanghuai Plain centered around this, the prelude of Chinese civilization was opened. As a result, Fuxi has become an epoch-making figure, who is respected by later generations as "the first of the three emperors" and "the first ancestor of Chinese humanity", and has become the ancestor of the Chinese nation, the Loong ancestor and the common ancestor of China. To commemorate

Fuxi's merits, a mausoleum temple was built in Huaiyang, where the Taihao Fuxi slept forever. Zhao Kuangyin, the Emperor Taizu of the Song Dynasty, set up a mausoleum temple, and since then there has been a fixed day for offering sacrifices. By the Ming and Qing Dynasties, it had been repaired and expanded repeatedly. Taihao Mausoleum was large in scale, brilliant and magnificent. This made the Taihaoling Temple Fair become ever more prosperous and lively.

During the temple fair, a variety of traditional folk entertainment activities are more attractive. Among them, juggling and performances are the most. Lion dancing, dragon lanterns, bamboo horses, dry boats and so on are all available. Compared with other temple fairs, the custom of Taihaoling Temple Fair has two very unique characteristics. One is "Danjingtiao", also known as "Danhualan", is the primitive dance of worshipping ancestors and pleasing gods. The other unique characteristic is the "mud dog" which can be seen everywhere in the temple fair. It is a kind of mud toy sold in the temple fair, and it can make a sound when was blown. According to textual research, these mud toys are living relics in the later period of primitive society. The folk activities of Taihaoling Temple Fair have many primitive cultural colors.

Today, the Taihaoling temple fair is more grand, and pilgrims have spread all over the country. During this period, many international scholars and friends also come to Taihao Mausoleum to explore ancient mysteries and study the oriental civilization of ancient Huaxia. The compatriots of Hong Kong, Macao and Taiwan and the descendants of overseas Chinese come to Taihao Mausoleum to search for their roots and ancestors every year. They are proud to pay homage to their ancestors in front of Fuxi Mausoleum, showing that they will never forget their ancestors and that they are descendants of the Loong.

第五章　新郑黄帝祭祖

　　黄帝故里拜祖大典，是自春秋战国以来华夏炎黄子孙于农历"三月三"在黄帝故里轩辕之丘（今河南省新郑市）祭拜先祖黄帝的仪式。唐代后升格为官方祭典。自 2006 年（农历丙戌年）开始，更名为"黄帝故里拜祖大典"。2008 年国务院确定新郑黄帝拜祖祭典为第一批国家级非物质文化遗产扩展项目。

　　郑州新郑古为有熊氏之国，轩辕黄帝农历三月三降于轩辕之丘，定都于有熊。黄帝一统天下，奠定中华，肇造文明，惜物爱民，被后人尊为中华人文始祖之一。春秋时代的历史典籍中就有三月三登新郑具茨山（俗称"始祖山"）朝拜黄帝的记载。唐代以后渐成规制，盛世时由官方主拜，乱世时由民间自办，一直绵延至今。

　　拜祖大典分为内广场（主要是海内外嘉宾和部分群众代表）和外广场（主要是当地群众和各类演职人员）。黄帝故里拜祖大典的议程固定为九项，分别是：盛世礼炮（21 响）、敬献花篮、净手上香、行施拜礼（主持人带领全体嘉宾一起行施拜礼）、恭读拜文、高唱颂歌（由著名歌星带领统一着装的男女青年和小学生一起高唱《黄帝颂》）、乐舞敬拜、祈福中华、天地人和。来自海内外的炎黄子孙都在这里焚香跪拜，寻根祭祖。

　　黄帝是中华民族的始祖，是所有海内外炎黄子孙公认的祖先。每年农历三月三，在河南新郑黄帝故里举办的拜祖大典活动，弘扬了中华优秀传统文化，突出了中华民族寻根拜祖的主题，象征炎黄子孙血脉相连、薪火相传。黄帝故里拜祖大典已经成为凝聚全球炎黄子孙的一个重要载体。祭拜黄帝在中国有悠久的历史传统，我们有理由将这一文化传统继承并发展下去，以增进海内外所有炎黄子孙对中华民族的认同、对中华优秀传统文化的认同。

Chapter 5
The Grand Ceremony of Worshipping Ancestor Huangdi in Xinzheng

The Grand Ceremony of Worshipping Ancestor in Huangdi's Hometown is a ceremony of worshiping ancestor Huangdi by the descendants of Yan and Huang of Chinese nation on the third day of the third lunar month at Xuanyuan Hill in the hometown of Huangdi (now Xinzheng, Henan Province), since the Spring and Autumn Period and the Warring States Period. After the Tang Dynasty, it was upgraded to an official ceremony. Since 2006 (the year of Bingxu in lunar calendar), it has been renamed to "the Grand Ceremony of Worshipping Ancestor in Huangdi's Hometown". In 2008, the State Council decided that the The Grand Ceremony of Worshipping Ancestor Huangdi in Xinzheng was the first batch of National Intangible Cultural Heritage Expansion Project.

Zhengzhou Xinzheng was a country of Youxiong clan in ancient times. Xuanyuan Huangdi was born on the third day of the third lunar month on Xuanyuan Hill and established the capital in Youxiong. The Huangdi unified the world, established China, created civilization, cherished things and loved the people, and was respected as one of the ancestors of Chinese culture by later generations. In the historical books of the Spring and Autumn Period, there are records of the pilgrimage to Huangdi on the third day of the third lunar month at Mount Juci (commonly known as the "ancestor mountain") in Xinzheng. After the Tang Dynasty, it gradually became a rule. In prosperous times, it was worshipped by the government, and in chaotic times, it was organized by the people, which has lasted till now.

The ceremony is divided into inner square (mainly for guests at home and abroad and some representatives of the masses), and outer square (mainly for local people and various performers). The agenda of the Grand Ceremony of Worshipping Ancestor in Huangdi's Hometown is fixed with nine items, namely: the grand age salute (21 gunshots), the sacrifice of flower basket, cleaning hands and offering incense, performing the worship ceremony (the host leads all guests to worship together), reading the worship text reverently, singing hymns loudly (the young men and women, and primary school students in same clothes led by famous singers sing the song of *Huangdi Ode*), music and dance worship, praying for China, praying for harmony between heaven, earth and humanity. The descendants of the Yan and Huang at home and abroad burned incense here, kneel down, seeking their roots and worshipping their ancestors.

Huangdi is the ancestor of the Chinese nation and is recognized by all descendants of the Yan and Huang at home and abroad. Every year on the third day of the third lunar month, the grand ceremony of worshipping ancestors held in the hometown of Huangdi in Xinzheng, Henan Province, promotes the excellent traditional culture of the Chinese nation, highlights the theme of the Chinese nation's seeking for roots and worshipping ancestors, symbolizes the blood ties of the descendants of Yan and Huang. The Grand Ceremony of Worshipping Ancestor in Huangdi's Hometown has become an important carrier for the cohesion of the descendants of Yan and Huang in the world. The worship of Huangdi has a long historical tradition in China. It is reasonable for us to inherit and develop this cultural tradition in order to enhance the identity of all the descendants of Yan and Huang at home and abroad towards the Chinese nation and towards the excellent traditional Chinese culture.

第六章　清明节

　　清明节是中国四大传统节日之一，祭祖扫墓是中原清明节习俗的中心内容。一到清明，人们就拿着祭品到墓地烧纸点烛，祭奠先祖。清明这天，各家门头要插柳枝，男女都戴柳环。2006 年，清明节被列入第一批国家级非物质文化遗产名录。

　　清明节气一般是在公历 4 月 5 日前后，即春分后第 15 日。清明节是节气与节日的结合体，源于上古时代的春祭，是天时与人时的合一。清明礼俗文化充分体现了"天人合一"的传统观念。

　　清明节也是中国重要的"时年八节"之一。清明处在生气旺盛、阴气衰退的时节，祭祖与踏青是清明节的两大礼俗主题。清明节的祭祖习俗，历代沿袭而成为中华民族一种固定的风俗。清明节扫墓祭祖的节俗传统自古延续不断，当今社会人们在清明节前后仍有上坟扫墓祭祖的习俗：铲除杂草，放上供品，于墓前上香祷祝、燃纸钱金锭等，又或简单地献上一束鲜花，以寄托对祖先的追念。

　　踏青为春日郊游，也称"踏春"，一般指初春时到郊外散步游玩。中华民族自古就有清明踏青的习俗。清明节的习俗除了踏青、祭祖之外，还在历史发展中吸收了荡秋千、踢蹴鞠、打马球、插柳等一系列风俗体育活动。

　　清明节是重大的传统春祭节日，扫墓祭祀、缅怀祖先，是中华民族数千年来留下的优良传统，不仅有利于弘扬孝道亲情、唤醒家族共同记忆，还可增强家族成员乃至民族的凝聚力和认同感。清明节不仅是人们祭祀祖先的节日，也是中华民族血脉精神和文化认同的纽带。

Chapter 6
The Qingming Festival

The Qingming Festival is one of the four traditional festivals in China, ancestor worshipping and tomb sweeping is the central content of the Qingming Festival in the Central Plains. As soon as the Qingming Festival comes, people take sacrifices to the cemetery and burn spirit money and light candles to commemorate their ancestors. On the day of the Qingming Festival, willow branches are inserted at the entrances of each household, and both men and women wear willow rings. In 2006, the Qingming Festival was listed in the first batch of National Intangible Cultural Heritage List.

The Qingming solar term is usually around the 5th of April, the 15th day after the Spring Equinox (Chunfen in Chinese). The Qingming Festival is a combination of solar term and festival. It originated from the ancient Spring Sacrificial Ceremony. The Qingming Festival combines the laws of nature with human activities. The Qingming ritual and custom culture fully embodies the traditional concept of "the harmony between nature and man".

The Qingming Festival is one of the eight important festivals in China. The Qingming Festival is in a period when "Yang Qi" is exuberant and "Yin Qi" is on the wane. Worshipping ancestors and going on a spring outing on the Qingming Festival are the two major themes of etiquette and custom. The custom of offering sacrifices to ancestors on the Qingming Festival has been a fixed custom of the Chinese nation in the past dynasties. The tradition of tomb-sweeping and ancestor-worshipping on the Qingming Festival has been going on since ancient times. In today's society, people still have the custom of tomb-sweeping and ancestor-worshipping during a period of the Qingming Festival: weeding eradication, placing offerings, offering prayers, burning incense, spirit money and gold ingots in front of the tomb, or simply presenting a bunch of flowers, in order to express our remembrance of ancestors.

Ta Qing (in Chinese) is a spring outing, also known as "Ta Chun"(in Chinese), which generally refers to take a walk in the countryside in the early spring. Since ancient times, the Chinese nation has had the custom of going on a spring outing in the Qingming Festival. In addition to going on a spring outing and worshipping ancestors, the Qingming Festival also absorbed a series of customs and sports activities such as swing, playing Cuju (kick the ball with the feet), playing polo, willow insertion and so on in its historical development.

The Qingming Festival is a major traditional spring sacrificial festival. Tomb-sweeping and ancestor-worshipping is a fine tradition left by the Chinese nation for thousands of years. It is not only conducive to promoting filial piety and family ties, awakening the common memory of the family, but also promoting the cohesion and identity of family members and even the nation. Qingming Festival is not only a festival for people to worship their ancestors, but also the bond of bloodline spirit and cultural identity for the Chinese nation.

第七章　端午节

端午节为每年农历五月初五，是中国四大传统节日之一。2006 年，端午节被列入首批国家级非物质文化遗产名录；自 2008 年起，被列为国家法定节假日。2009 年 9 月，联合国教科文组织正式批准将端午节列入人类非物质文化遗产代表作名录，端午节成为中国首个入选人类非遗的节日。

端午节起源于中国，最初是上古先民以龙舟竞渡形式祭祀龙祖的节日。因战国时期的楚国诗人屈原在端午节跳汨罗江自尽，后亦将端午节作为纪念屈原的节日；个别地方也有纪念伍子胥、曹娥及介子推的说法。总的来说，端午节起源于龙图腾祭祀，因北方把端午视为"恶月恶日"，于是为端午节注入了夏季时令"祛病防疫"风尚，后又增加了纪念屈原等历史人物的内容，形成如今端午节的文化内涵。

包粽子、吃粽子是中原端午节一项重要的民俗活动。河南人不仅要吃粽子，还要吃油炸食品。像油条、麻花、麻叶等，都是端午节常做的油炸食品。在众多的油炸食品中，糖糕和菜角是最典型、最有代表性的节日食品。在端午节这天，有些人家还讲究吃鸡蛋。

古代端午节捉癞蛤蟆的风俗现在仍在河南农村地区流行。民间认为，癞蛤蟆的毒液能够清热解毒，特别是端午这天捉到的蛤蟆毒性最大、质量最好。

端午节这天，大人给孩子们戴上五毒肚兜，穿上黄色绣花鞋，手、脚系上五色彩线，脖子上佩戴精美漂亮的香囊，以此避邪、保佑孩子平安。

　　端午习俗体现了中国古人"天人合一"的自然观，反映了源远流长、博大精深的中华文化内涵。

Chapter 7
The Dragon Boat Festival

The Dragon Boat Festival, the fifth day of the fifth month in the lunar calendar, is one of the four traditional festivals in China. In 2006, the Dragon Boat Festival was listed in the first batch of National Intangible Cultural Heritage List; since 2008, it has been listed as a national holiday. In September 2009, UNESCO officially approved the inclusion of the Dragon Boat Festival in the Representative List of the Intangible Cultural Heritage of Humanity. The Dragon Boat Festival became the first festival in China to be selected as the world's intangible cultural heritage.

The Dragon Boat Festival, which originated in China, was originally a festival in which ancient ancestors sacrificed to the Dragon God in the form of dragon boat racing. Because Qu Yuan, a poet of the State of Chu in the Warring States Period, committed suicide by jumping into the Miluo River on this day, the Dragon Boat Festival also became a festival to commemorate Qu Yuan. In some places, there are also statements commemorating Wu Zixu, Cao E and Jie Zitui. Generally speaking, the Dragon Boat Festival originated from Dragon totem worship. Cause it was regarded as the "bad month and bad day" in the north, it was injected into the fashion of "dispelling disease and preventing epidemic disease" in summer season. It also added the elements related to historical figures such as Quyuan, and finally formed the cultural connotation of today's Dragon Boat Festival.

Wrapping Zongzi and eating Zongzi are important folk activities on the Dragon Boat Festival in the Central Plains. Henan people not only eat Zongzi, but also eat fried food. Like deep-fried dough sticks, fried dough twist, twisted leaves and so on, they are fried foods that people often make on the Dragon Boat Festival. Among many fried foods, fried sugar cakes and deep-fried vegetable dumplings are the most typical and representative festival foods. On the Dragon Boat Festival, some people are even particular about eating eggs.

The custom of catching toads on the Dragon Boat Festival in ancient times is still popular in Henan rural areas. It is believed that toads' venom can clear away heat and detoxify toxins. Especially the toads caught on the Dragon Boat Festival are the most toxic and of the best quality.

On the Dragon Boat Festival, adults dress their children with five poisonous bellybands, yellow embroidered shoes, five-color threads on hands and feet, and beautiful sachets around their necks to avoid evil and protect their children.

The Dragon Boat Festival custom embodies the Chinese ancients' natural view of "harmony between nature and human", and reflects the extensive and profound connotation of Chinese culture with a long history.

第八章　七夕节

七夕节，又名七巧节、乞巧节，是一个以"牛郎织女"民间传说为载体，以爱情为主题，以女性为主体的综合性节日。七夕节发源于中国，受中华文化影响的亚洲国家如日本、朝鲜、越南等也有庆祝七夕的传统。2006年，七夕节被列入第一批国家级非物质文化遗产名录。

七夕节始于汉代，在古代也被称为乞巧节，它是中国古代的妇女节。在三四千年前，随着人们对自然科学和天文的认识逐渐深入，出现了关于牵牛星和织女星的记载。后来随着古代诗人在诗中的引用和歌颂、牛郎织女爱情故事的融入，民间女子更加重视七夕。随着人类历史的发展，七夕节也变成了中国情人节。

七夕节是世界上最早的爱情节日之一。七夕夜晚坐看牵牛织女星、访闺中密友、拜祭织女、祈祷姻缘、切磋女红、乞巧祈福等，是中国民间的传统七夕习俗。相传，在每年的这个夜晚，是天上织女与牛郎在鹊桥相会之时，抬头可以看到牛郎织女在银河相会，在瓜果架下可偷听到两人在天上相会时的绵绵情话。牛郎和织女的故事最早在南北朝的时候出现，到了唐宋时期受到广大文人墨客的称颂，后来在民间广为流传。凡间的女孩们在这个充满浪漫气息的晚上，对着天空的朗朗明月，摆上时令瓜果，朝天祭拜，乞求天上的织女能赋予她们聪慧的心灵和灵巧的双手，让自己的针织女红技法娴熟，更乞求爱情婚姻的姻缘巧配。过去，婚姻对于女性来说是决定一生幸福与否的终身大事，所以，世间无数的有情男女都会在这个晚上夜深人静时，对着星空祈祷自己的姻缘美满。

Chapter 8
The Qixi Festival

The Qixi Festival, also known as Qiqiao Festival and Festival of Praying for Wisdom and Ingenuity, is a comprehensive festival with "Cowherd and Weaver Girl" folklore as the carrier, love as the theme and women as the main participants. The Qixi Festival originated in China. Asian countries affected by Chinese culture, such as Japan, Korea and Vietnam, also have the tradition of celebrating the Qixi Festival. In 2006, the Qixi Festival was listed in the first batch of National Intangible Cultural Heritage List.

The Qixi Festival, which began in the Han Dynasty, was also called Qiqiao Festival in ancient times. It was the Women's Festival in ancient China. Around three or four thousand years ago, as Chinese people's understanding of natural science and astronomy gradually deepened, records about Altair and Vega emerged. Later, with the quotation and praise of ancient poets in the poems, and the integration of the love story of Cowherd and Weaver Girl, the folk women paid more attention to the Qixi Festival. With the development of human history, the Qixi Festival has become Chinese Valentine's Day.

The Qixi Festival is one of the earliest love festivals in the world. Sitting and watching Altair and Vega, visiting close friends in the boudoir, worshipping the Weaver Girl, praying for marriage, consulting the needlework, begging for luck and ingenuity and so on are the traditional Chinese customs of the Qixi Festival. According to legend, on this night of every year, the Weaver Girl and the Cowherd meet at the Magpie Bridge in the sky, when looking up, one can witness the meeting of the Cowherd and the Weaver Girl across the Milky Way; under the melon and fruit trellises, one can overhear the affectionate whispers of the Cowherd and the Weaver Girl when they meet in the sky. The story of the Cowherd and the Weaver Girl first appeared in the Southern and Northern Dynasties, and was praised by literati and scholars in the Tang and Song Dynasties. Later, it was widely spread among the people. On this romantic evening, the girls in the world offer fruits and melons in season to the bright moon in the sky, pray to the Weaver Girl to give them wisdom and dexterous hands, to make their knitting skills proficient, and to beg for the marriage of love. In the past, marriage used to be a life-long event for women to decide whether they would be happy or not, so countless affectionate men and women in the world would pray for their marriage in the dark of the night, facing the stars.

第九章 中元节

中元节，又称施孤、鬼节、斋孤、地官节，节日习俗主要有祭祖、放河灯、祀亡魂、焚纸锭等。中元节是流行于汉字文化圈及海外华人圈的传统文化节日，与除夕、清明节、重阳节一样，均是中华民族传统的祭祖大节。2010 年，中元节被列入国家级非物质文化遗产名录。

中元节由上古时代"七月半"农作物丰收秋尝祭祖演变而来。"七月半"被称为"中元节"，则是源于东汉后道教的说法。道教认为七月半是地官诞辰，祈求地官赦罪之日，阴曹地府将放出全部鬼魂，已故祖先可回家团圆；在佛教中称为"盂兰盆节"。在统治者推崇道教的唐代，中元节开始兴盛，并且逐渐将"中元"固定为节名相沿迄今。

中元节民间俗信行为中，最为突出的是烧纸。据传说，阳间的纸就是阴间的钱，人们烧纸就是给亡故的先辈亲人送钱。通常上坟烧纸时要留下几张，到十字路口焚烧，目的是给无家可归的野鬼一些施舍，它们就不会去抢劫送给祖先的钱了。古时候，商丘县在中元节时，人们会悬挂纸旗于门口，传说可以防虫；孟津县在中元节有放风筝的习俗；郏县七月十五时，民间流行在门前画一灰圈，在圈内焚烧纸以祭拜祖先。

中元节亦有禁忌：床头忌挂风铃，风铃容易招来鬼魂，而睡觉的时候是最容易被鬼魂"入侵"的时刻；忌夜游，八字轻的人尽量不要夜游；忌非特定场合烧冥纸；忌偷吃祭品，这些是属于鬼魂的食物；忌乱踩冥纸，冥纸是献给鬼魂的祭品。

中元节是中国传统祭祖节日之一，蕴含着中国人追怀先人的文化传统，其文化背后体现的是古人"慎终追远"的思想，其文化核心是敬祖尽孝。

Chapter 9
The Zhongyuan Festival

The Zhongyuan Festival, also known as Shigu, Ghost Festival, Zhaigu, Diguan Festival in Chinese, festival customs mainly include offering sacrifices to ancestors, floating river lanterns, worshipping the spirits of the deceased, and burning paper ingots, etc. Zhongyuan Festival is a traditional cultural festival, popular in Chinese culture circles and overseas Chinese, same as New Year's Eve, the Qingming Festival and the Double Ninth Festival are the traditional ancestor worship festivals of the Chinese nation. In 2010, the Zhongyuan Festival was selected in the National Intangible Cultural Heritage List.

The Zhongyuan Festival evolved from the ancient "July and a half" of harvest and autumn sacrifice to ancestors. "July and a half" is called "Zhongyuan Festival", which originated from Taoism after the Eastern Han Dynasty. Taoism believes that July and a half is the birthday of the Diguan (the god who manages ghosts in Chinese), also the day praying for forgiveness of the Diguan, the underworld will release all ghosts, and the deceased ancestors can go home to reunite; in Buddhism it is known as the "Obon (Yulanpen Festival in Chinese)". In the Tang Dynasty, when the rulers respected Taoism, Zhongyuan Festival began to flourish, gradually fixed "Zhongyuan" as a festival name and it has continued ever since.

In the Zhongyuan Festival, the most prominent folk custom is burning spirit money. According to the legend, paper in the mortal world is money in the netherworld, and people burn it to send money to their deceased ancestors. Usually when burning paper in front of the grave, several pieces of paper are left to burn at the crossroads. The purpose is to give some alms to the homeless wild ghosts, then they will not rob ancestors of money. In ancient times, during the Zhongyuan Festival in Shangqiu County, paper flags were hung at the doorway, it was said that they can prevent insects. People in Mengjin County flied kites in Zhongyuan Festival. On the fifteenth day of the seventh lunar month, it was popular in Jia County that people drew a gray circle in front of the door and burnt spirit money in the circle to worship ancestors.

The Zhongyuan Festival also has some taboos: forbidding hanging wind bells at the bedside, because wind bells are easy to attract ghosts, and sleeping time is the most vulnerable time to be "invaded"; forbidding night travel, people with a weak Bazi try not to go out at night as much as possible; forbidding burning ghost paper on non-specific occasions; forbidding eating sacrifices, which belong to ghosts; forbidding trampling on paper dedicated to, which is ghost's sacrifices.

The Zhongyuan Festival is one of the traditional Chinese ancestor worship festivals, it embodies the cultural tradition of Chinese people in commemorating their ancestors, and its culture reflects the ancients' thought of "cherishing the memory of one's ancestors with solemnity and respect", its cultural core is the respect for their ancestors and filial piety.

第十章　中秋节

农历八月十五中秋节，源于古代中原地区的祭月迎寒活动，是与春节齐名的中国传统节日之一。受中华文化的影响，中秋节也是东亚和东南亚一些国家和地区的人，尤其是当地的华人华侨的传统节日。2006 年，中秋节被列入首批国家级非物质文化遗产名录。

作为节日，中秋节在西汉时已初具雏形。晋时已有赏月之举。唐朝时，传说唐玄宗梦游月宫，得到了《霓裳羽衣曲》，民间开始盛行过中秋节的习俗；唐朝以后，中秋节才成为固定的节日。到北宋时正式定名中秋节。明清时期，中秋节已经成为中国的一大传统节日，至今长盛不衰。中秋节自古便有祭月、赏月、拜月、吃月饼、赏桂花、饮桂花酒等习俗。中秋节以月圆寄托思念故乡、思念亲人、祈盼丰收和幸福的情感，成为丰富多彩、弥足珍贵的文化遗产。

铁塔燃灯是开封地区中秋节的一项重要活动，是开封人民自汉代沿袭下来的习俗。铁塔所在的开宝寺（明代以后人们称为铁塔寺），景色优美，是佛事活动的重要场所，也是人们的游乐苑圃。汤阴地区过去家家都要蒸月饼（白面里面放糖，蒸成圆饼状，再用木梳、顶针一类的工具按上几个图案），待中秋夜月上树梢时，人们开始用月饼、水果之类供奉月亮。南阳地区旧时中秋节夜设茶果、月饼于庭院，焚香祭月，称为"圆月"，以示秋季丰收、合家团圆之意。在巩义，节前人们向亲友馈送月饼，寓意全家团圆；晚上在院内设案，摆上月饼、水果等供品，面向月亮许愿，这叫"愿月"。此外，在驻马店地区，八月十五有吃糍粑和月饼的风俗。

中秋节是我国四大传统节日之一。传统节日文化的寻根，对继承中华文化优良传统、建设和谐社会，乃至营造健康的节日氛围有着一定的启迪意义。

Chapter 10
The Mid–Autumn Festival

The Mid-Autumn Festival on the fifteenth day of the eighth month of the lunar calendar, which originated from the activities of offering sacrifices to the moon and greeting the cold in the ancient Central Plains, is one of the Chinese traditional festivals as famous as the Spring Festival. Influenced by Chinese culture, Mid-Autumn Festival is also a traditional festival for overseas people in some countries and regions in East and Southeast Asian, especially for the local Chinese. In 2006, the Mid-Autumn Festival was listed in the first batch of National Intangible Cultural Heritage List.

As a festival, the Mid-Autumn Festival had its embryonic form in the Western Han Dynasty. In Jin Dynasty, it had the act of admiring the moon. Legend has it that Emperor Xuanzong in Tang Dynasty sleepwalking in the Moon Palace and getting the *Melody of Raiment of Rainbows and Feathers*, the custom of Mid-Autumn Festival began to prevail among the people. After the Tang Dynasty, the Mid-Autumn Festival became a fixed festival. By the Northern Song Dynasty, the Mid-Autumn Festival was officially named. In the Ming and Qing Dynasties, the Mid-Autumn Festival had become a major traditional festival in China, and it had been flourishing ever since. Since ancient times, the Mid-Autumn Festival has the customs of offering sacrifices to the moon, admiring the moon, worshipping the moon, eating mooncakes, enjoying osmanthus flowers, drinking osmanthus wine and so on. The roundness of the full moon during Mid-Autumn Festival represents the sentiments of longing for one's homeland and loved one, hope for harvest and happiness. It has become a rich and precious cultural heritage.

Lighting the Iron Tower is an important activity of the Mid-Autumn Festival in Kaifeng area, it is a custom inherited by Kaifeng people from the Han Dynasty. The Kaibao Temple (known as the Iron Tower Temple after the Ming Dynasty), where the Iron Tower is located, has beautiful scenery. It is an important place for Buddhist activities and a recreational garden for people. People in Tangyin used to steam mooncakes at home (put sugar in white flour, steam into round cakes, with several patterns made by wooden combs, thimbles and other tools) in the past. On the Mid-Autumn night, when the moon rose up to tree's top, mooncakes and fruits were used to worship the moon. In Nanyang, tea, fruits and mooncakes were set up in the courtyard on Mid-Autumn Festival night and incense was burned to offer sacrifices to the moon in the past, which was called the "Yuan Yue (full moon)" to show the harvest of autumn and the reunion of the family. In Gongyi, mooncakes are given to relatives and friends before the Mid-Autumn Festival, symbolizing the whole family reunion. In the evening, a table is set up in the courtyard, offering mooncakes, fruits and so on, to make a wish to the moon, which is called the "Wishing Moon". In addition, in Zhumadian, there is a custom to eat glutinous rice cake and mooncakes on the fifteenth day of the eighth lunar month.

The Mid-Autumn Festival is one of the four traditional festivals in China. Searching for the root of traditional festival culture has certain enlightenment significance for inheriting the fine tradition of Chinese culture, building a harmonious society, and even creating a healthy festival atmosphere.

第十一章　重阳节

农历九月初九，是我国传统节日重阳节。《易经》中把"九"定为阳数，"九九"两阳数相重，故曰"重阳"。1989 年，农历九月九日被定为"敬老节"，倡导全社会树立尊老、敬老、爱老、助老的风气。2006 年，重阳节被列入首批国家级非物质文化遗产名录。

重阳节起始于上古，成形于春秋战国时期，普及于西汉，鼎盛于唐代以后。唐代是传统节日习俗糅合定型的重要时期，重阳节在唐代形成的主体部分传承至今。

古人认为"九"是吉利的数字，把它作为阳数。九月初九，占了两个九字，双阳相重，所以人们都叫它"重九"或"重阳"。在这一天，有出游、登高、望远、插茱萸、饮菊花酒等避灾避难的风俗，故又称"登高节"。另外，在中原人的传统观念中，"双九"蕴含生命长久、健康长寿的意义。这一天还有许多以老人为中心的尊老、爱老、敬老活动。因此，登高赏秋与感恩敬老是当今重阳节活动的两大重要主题。除此还有秋游赏菊、佩插茱萸、拜神祭祖及饮宴求寿等习俗。

现在，河南民间重阳节赏菊的活动越来越盛行。因为菊花多在农历九月开放，观赏菊花成为重阳节的一项重要内容。

2010 年中国民间文艺家协会授予南阳市西峡县"中国重阳文化之乡"的称号，并在西峡建立了全国唯一的"中国重阳文化研究中心"，每年农历九月九日这里都会举办"中国·西峡重阳文化节"。

重阳节在历史发展演变中杂糅多种民俗于一体，承载了丰富的文化内涵，与除夕、清明节、中元节并称中国传统四大祭祖节日。

Chapter 11
The Double Ninth Festival

The ninth day of ninth month in the lunar calendar is the traditional Double Ninth Festival in China. In *the Book of Changes*, "Nine" is defined as a positive/lucky number ("Yang" number in Chinese), and double "Nine", is called "Chongyang". In 1989, ninth day of ninth month of the lunar calendar was designated as "Respect for the Aged Day", advocating the whole society to establish a culture of respecting, revering, loving and helping the elderly. In 2006, the Double Ninth Festival was listed in the first batch of National Intangible Cultural Heritage List.

The Double Ninth Festival originated in ancient times, took shape during the Spring and Autumn Period and the Warring States Period, popularized in the Western Han Dynasty, and flourished after the Tang Dynasty. Tang Dynasty is an important period in which traditional festival customs are combined and finalized. Main part of the Double Ninth Festival formed in Tang Dynasty has been inherited until now.

The ancients believed that "nine" was a lucky number and regarded it as a Yang number. The ninth day of ninth lunar month, occupies two ninth characters, and the Yang are double, so people call it "Double Ninth" or "Double Yang". On this day, there are traveling, climbing mountains, looking into the distance, wearing dogwood, drinking chrysanthemum wine and other customs to avoid disaster, so it is also known as "Climbing Mountains Festival". In addition, in the traditional concept of the Central Plains people, "Double Nine" contains the meaning of health and longevity. On this day, there are many activities of respecting, loving and revering the elderly centered on the Aged. Therefore, climbing high to appreciate autumn and showing gratitude and respect for the elderly are two important themes of the Double Ninth Festival activities. In addition, there are Autumn outing to appreciate chrysanthemums, wearing dogwood, worshipping gods and ancestors and holding feast for longevity and other customs.

Nowadays, the activities of appreciating chrysanthemums on the Double Ninth Festival are more and more popular in Henan. Because most chrysanthemums are blooming in ninth lunar month, appreciating chrysanthemums has become an important part of the festival.

In 2010, the Chinese Folk Literature and Art Association granted Xixia County of Nanyang City as the "Town of Chinese Chongyang Culture" and established the only "Research Center of Chinese Chongyang Culture" in Xixia. Every year, the "China Xixia Chongyang Cultural Festival" is held here on the ninth day of ninth month of the lunar calendar.

The Double Ninth Festival is a blend of various folk customs in the historical development and evolution, which carries rich cultural connotations. The Double Ninth Festival, Chinese New Year's Eve, Qingming Festival, and Zhongyuan Festival are also known as the four traditional Chinese ancestor worship festivals.

第十二章　冬至节

冬至，俗称"冬节"。冬至兼具自然与人文两大内涵，既是二十四节气中一个重要的节气，也是中华民族的重要传统节日。冬至被视为冬季的大节日，在古代民间有"冬至大如年"的说法。冬至的节日习俗传承已近3000年，是中华民族宝贵的非物质文化遗产。

冬至过节源于汉代，盛于唐宋，相沿至今。古人对冬至十分重视，人们认为冬至是阴阳二气的自然转化，是上天赐予的福气。

关于冬至的民俗有很多。从周代起冬至日就有祈福活动，目的在于祈求消除疫疾，减少荒年及人民的饥饿与死亡。汉朝以冬至为"冬节"，官府要举行祝贺仪式，称为"贺冬"；"冬节"朝廷上下要放假休息，亲朋各以美食相赠，相互拜访，欢乐地过一个"安身静体"的节日。唐宋时期，冬至是祭天祀祖的日子，皇帝在这天要到郊外举行祭天大典，百姓在这一天要向父母尊长祭拜。明清两代，皇帝均有祭天大典，谓之"冬至郊天"。宫内有百官向皇帝呈递贺表的仪式，还要互相投刺祝贺，就像元旦一样。古人认为自冬至起，天地阳气开始兴作渐强，冬至一阳生、天地阳气回升，所以古人将冬至视为吉日，是冬季祭祖大节。

关于冬至饮食，北方普遍吃水饺。每年农历冬至这天，不论贫富，饺子是必不可少的节日饭。谚云："十月一，冬至到，家家户户吃水饺。"这种习俗，是为纪念"医圣"张仲景冬至舍药留下的。冬至吃饺子，是不忘"医圣"张仲景"祛寒娇耳汤"之恩。至今南阳仍有"冬至不端饺子碗，冻掉耳朵没人管"的民谣。

Chapter 12
The Winter Solstice Festival

The Winter Solstice Festival is commonly known as the "Winter Festival". The Winter Solstice Festival has two connotations of nature and humanity. It is not only an important solar term in the 24 solar terms, but also a momentous traditional festival of the Chinese nation. The Winter Solstice Festival is regarded as a big festival in winter. In ancient times, there was a saying that "Winter Solstice is as important as the Spring Festival". Its festival customs have been passed down for nearly 3000 years, and it is a valuable intangible cultural heritage of the Chinese nation.

The Winter Solstice Festival originated in the Han Dynasty, flourished in the Tang and Song Dynasties, and has been passed down to this day. The ancients attached great importance to the Winter Solstice Festival. It is believed that the Winter Solstice Festival is a natural transformation of Yin and Yang, and a blessing from heaven.

There are many customs about the Winter Solstice Festival. Since the Zhou Dynasty, there have been prayer activities aimed at praying for eliminating epidemics, reducing famine and people's hunger and death. In the Han Dynasty, the Winter Solstice Festival was the "Winter Festival". The imperial government held a congratulation ceremony called "Winter Congratulations". The court had to take a holiday and rest on that day. The relatives and friends gave each other delicious food, visited each other and had a happy "rest" festival. In the Tang and Song Dynasties, the Winter Solstice Festival was a day to worship the heavens and ancestors. On that day, the emperor would go to the suburbs to hold a heaven worship ceremony, ordinary people would worship their parents and elders. In the Ming and Qing Dynasties, the emperors held heaven worship ceremonies, which were called "Winter Solstice Jiao Tian". There were ceremonies in the palace where all officials presented congratulations to the emperor, and they also had to send name card to congratulate each other just like New Year's Day. The ancients believed that since the Winter Solstice Festival, the Yang Qi of heaven and earth began to grow stronger and stronger, and the Yang Qi of heaven and earth rebounded during the Winter Solstice Festival. Therefore, the ancients regarded the Winter Solstice as a lucky day and a winter festival to worship ancestors.

As for the Winter Solstice Festival diet, dumplings are commonly eaten in the north. On the Winter Solstice Festival of the lunar calendar every year, dumplings are the indispensable festival meal for the rich and poor. The proverb says, "When the Winter Solstice Festival comes on the first day of the tenth lunar month, every household eats dumplings." This custom was left in memory of the Medical Sage Zhang Zhongjing's act of distributing medicine on the Winter Solstice Festival. Eating dumplings during the Winter Solstice Festival is not forgetting the kindness of Zhang Zhongjing's Cold-Dispelling Jiao'er Soup (a lamb and herbal soup with ear-shaped dough pockets, to treat frost bitten ears of the poor, today known as Jiaozi/dumplings). Up to now, Nanyang still has a folk song that "dumpling bowls are not served during the Winter Solstice Festival, ears will be frozen and nobody cares about them".

第十三章　腊八节

　　农历腊月初八，是我国汉族传统的腊八节，这天我国大多数地区都有吃腊八粥的习俗。相传这一天是佛教创始人释迦牟尼在菩提树下成道并创立佛教的日子，故又被称为"成道节"。在河南，腊八粥又称"大家饭"，是纪念岳飞的一种节日食俗。

　　自上古时代起，就有在腊日祭祀祖先和神灵（包括门神、户神、宅神、灶神、井神）的习俗，祈求丰收和吉祥。南北朝时期，腊日才固定在腊月初八，后来佛教文化也加入其中，经历代演变，逐渐成为家喻户晓的民间节日。

　　腊八节也寄托了人们对忠臣岳飞的怀念。当年，岳飞率部抗金于朱仙镇，正值数九严冬，岳家军衣食不济、挨饿受冻，众百姓相继送粥，岳家军饱餐了一顿百姓送的"千家粥"，结果大胜而归。这天正是腊月初八。岳飞就义后，人们为了纪念他，每到腊月初八，便以杂粮豆果煮粥，终于成俗。

　　腊八节喝腊八粥的习俗由来已久。过去各寺院都在腊八节这天用香谷和果实做成粥来赠送给门徒和善男信女们。传说喝了这种粥以后，就可以得到佛祖的保佑，因此，腊八粥也叫"福寿粥""福德粥"和"佛粥"。腊八粥用八种当年收获的新鲜粮食和瓜果煮成，一般都为甜味粥。而中原地区的许多农家却喜欢吃咸腊八粥，粥内除大米、小米、绿豆、豇豆、花生、红枣、核桃、莲子、桂圆、百合等原料外，还要加萝卜、白菜、粉条、海带、豆腐等。腊八粥的食料都有民俗谐音，例如：红枣花生比喻早生贵子，核桃表示和和美美，莲子象征恩爱连心，桂圆寓意富贵团圆，百合意为百事和睦，等等，人们以此期盼未来生活的美好。腊八粥熬好之后，要先敬神祭祖；之后要赠送亲友，一定要在中午之前送出去；最后才是全家人食用。

Chapter 13
The Laba Festival

The eighth day of the twelfth lunar month is the traditional Laba Festival of the Han nationality in China. On this day, most areas in China have the custom of eating Laba porridge. According to legend, this day is when Sakyamuni, the founder of Buddhism, established Buddhism under Bodhi Tree, so it is also known as the "Cheng Dao Festival (Enlightenment Day)". In Henan Province, Laba porridge, also known as "Da Jia Meal (in Chinese)", is a festival food custom in memory of Yue Fei.

Since ancient times, there has been a custom of offering sacrifices to ancestors and gods (including door gods, household gods, house gods, kitchen gods, well gods) in La Day (one of the days in the twelfth lunar month) to pray for good harvest and good luck. In the Northern and Southern Dynasties, La Day was fixed on the eighth day of twelfth lunar month. Later, Buddhist culture was incorporated into the La Day. La Day has evolved from generation to generation and gradually become a well-known folk festival.

The Laba Festival also embodies people's memories of Yue Fei, a loyal minister. In that year, Yue Fei's army resisted Jin's army in Zhuxian Town, which was in the severe and bitter winter. Yue's army was poor in clothing and food, hungry and frozen. People sent porridge to them one after another. Yue's army had a full meal of "Porridge of a Thousand Homes" from the people, and the result was a great victory. It was the eighth day of twelfth lunar month. After Yue Fei's death, in memory of him, the people cooked porridge with miscellaneous grains, beans and fruits on the eighth day of twelfth lunar month, and it finally became a custom.

The custom of eating Laba porridge on the Laba Festival has a long history. In the past, various monasteries made porridge from fragrant grains and fruit to give to disciples and believers on that day. Legend has it that after eating this porridge, you can get the blessing of Buddha. Therefore, Laba porridge is also called "Fushou porridge", "Fude porridge" and "Buddha porridge". Laba porridge is boiled with eight kinds of fresh grains and fruits harvested in that year, it is generally sweet porridge. However, many farmers in the Central Plains like to eat salty Laba porridge, which contains not only rice, millet, mung beans, cowpea, peanut, jujube, walnut, lotus seed, longan, lily and other raw materials, but also radish, cabbage, vermicelli, kelp, tofu and so on. Laba porridge food has folk homonyms, such as: jujube and peanut analogize "zao sheng gui zi" (Have a lovely baby soon), walnut symbolizes harmony, lotus seed symbolizes love, longan symbolizes wealth and reunion, lily also symbolizes harmony and so on. People hope for a better life in the future by eating these foods. After Laba porridge is boiled, we must first offer it to god and ancestors as a form of worship. After that, you must give it to your relatives and friends before noon. Finally, the whole family can enjoy Laba porridge together.

第十四章　祭灶节

　　农历腊月二十三，是春节前的一个重要民间节日，人们称它为"祭灶节"。祭灶节在我国民俗中历史悠久，是中华民族的传统节日，也被称为小年、灶王节等。祭灶节也被视为过年的开端，人们在祭灶日要回家团圆，吃麻糖，向灶神祈福，以求全家来年平安。

　　祭灶是一个在中国民间影响很大、流传极广的传统习俗。中国古代奉祀的灶神，有一种说法是火神祝融。古时先民在没有火的时候过着茹毛饮血的日子，后来人们会使用火才享受到更多的人间美味，所以自古以来人们对火和火神祝融都有着神圣的敬畏感，先人们祭灶也和这有着千丝万缕的联系。

　　祭灶的传统在中国民间信仰中俗称"送神"。据说每年年底，灶君、太岁神与民间诸神都要回天庭向玉皇大帝述职，尤其灶君会向玉帝禀告人间善恶是非，作为对人类奖惩报应的依据，故人们大多在此时奉拜家中诸神与灶君。

　　祭灶仪式多在晚上进行。祭灶时，祭灶人跪在灶王爷像前，怀抱公鸡。也有人让孩子抱鸡跪于大人之后。据说鸡是灶王爷升天所骑之马，故鸡不称为鸡，而称为马。若是红公鸡，俗称"红马"；白公鸡，俗称"白马"。焚烧香表后，男主人斟酒叩头，进行祝祷；之后，祭灶人高喊一声："领！"并执酒浇鸡头。若鸡扑棱有声，说明灶爷已经领情；若鸡纹丝不动，还需再浇。祭灶仪式结束后，人们开始食用灶糖和火烧等祭灶食品，有的地方还要吃糖糕、油饼，喝豆腐汤。

在河南，人们把祭灶节看作仅次于中秋的团圆节。凡在外地工作、经商、上学的人，都会争取在腊月二十三之前赶回家里。相传能吃到家里做的祭灶火烧，便会得到灶神的保护，来年家人就能平安无事。

Chapter 14
The Kitchen God Festival

The twenty-third day of the twelfth lunar month is an important folk festival before the Spring Festival. People call it the "Kitchen God Festival". The Kitchen God Festival, with a long history in Chinese folklore, is a traditional festival of the Chinese nation. It is also known as Xiaonian and Kitchen God's Day. The Kitchen God Festival is also regarded as the beginning of the Spring Festival. People will go home to reunite on the Kitchen God Festival, eat sesame candy and pray for the blessing of the Kitchen God for the safety of the whole family in the coming year.

Worshipping the Kitchen God is a traditional custom with great influence and wide spread among Chinese people. There is a saying that the Kitchen God worshipped in ancient China is Zhurong, the God of Fire. In ancient times, the ancestors lived a life of eating raw meat and drinking blood without fire. Later, people learned to use fire to enjoy more delicacies of the world, so people had a sense of sacred awe for fire and the God of Fire since ancient times. The ancestors offered sacrifices to Kitchen God which is also closely related to this.

The tradition of offering sacrifices to Kitchen God is commonly called "sending gods" in Chinese folk beliefs. It is said that at the end of each year, Kitchen God, Tai Sui God and folk gods will return to heaven to report their duties to the Jade Emperor. In particular, Kitchen God will inform the Jade Emperor of the good and evil in the world, as a basis for rewards and punishments for human beings, so people mostly worship the family gods and Kitchen God at this time.

Most of the ceremonies are held at night. When worshipping the Kitchen God, people kneel in front of the image of the Kitchen God, embracing the cock. Others let children kneel behind adults with cock in their arms. It is said that the cock is the horse on which the Kitchen God ascends to heaven. Hence, the cock is not called a cock, but a horse. If it is a red cock, it is commonly known as "red horse"; white cock, commonly known as "white horse". After burning incense, the man poured liquor and kowtowed, and read words in his mouth. After praying, the man who worshipped the Kitchen God shouts: "Ling! (in Chinese)" and then pours the cock head with liquor. If the cock flutters with sounds, it shows that the Kitchen God has appreciated it. If the cock doesn't move, it needs to be watered again. After the ceremony, people began to eat sticky candy, baked wheat cake and other food for sacrifice to the Kitchen God, in some places also eat sugar cakes, oil cakes and tofu soup.

In Henan Province, people regard the Kitchen God Festival as the reunion festival which is second only to the Mid-Autumn Festival. All those who work, do business and go to school outside strive to get home before the twenty-third day of the twelfth lunar month. It's said that if you can eat the sacrificial baked wheat cake made at home, you will be protected by the Kitchen God, and your family will be safe and sound in the coming year.

第十五章　除夕

　　除夕是年尾的最后一个晚上，因常在农历腊月廿九或三十，故又称该日为大年三十。除夕是除旧迎新、阖家团圆、祭祀祖先的日子，与清明节、中元节、重阳节同为中国民间传统的祭祖大节。受中华文化的影响，除夕也是汉文化圈国家及世界各地华人华侨的传统节日。

　　除夕是春节的前夜，又叫年三十。传说古时候有个凶恶的怪兽叫夕，每到岁末便出来害人。后来，人们知道夕最怕红色和声响，于是年三十晚上，家家户户贴红春联、燃放爆竹来驱除夕兽，以求新一年的安宁。这种习俗从此流传下来，年三十晚上便称为除夕了。

　　宋代被后人视为中国古代传统文化的顶峰时期。宋代除夕礼俗，在沿袭周秦汉唐相关礼俗的基础上，又有与时俱进的变革和创新之处。宋代除夕前夕的买卖节日物品、君臣亲友间馈赠礼品、清洁卫生、贴门神、祭祖、燃放爆竹等除夕礼俗活动，均具有浓郁的时代特色。

　　除夕自古就有祭祖、守岁、吃团圆饭、贴年红、挂灯笼等习俗，流传至今，经久不息。很多地方有除夕这一天进行大扫除的习俗，过了除夕迎来春节就不能再动笤帚了，人们认为那样会赶走福气。除夕那天最大的事情就是贴春联，买好春联、财神像、窗花等，贴在家里的门窗上，寓意来年福气满满、快乐多多。除夕之夜，全家人在一起吃"年夜饭"，有一家人团聚过年的味道。吃过年夜饭，就是守岁。除夕守岁是最重要的年俗活动之一，守岁之俗由来已久。守岁的民俗主要表现为除夕夜灯火通宵不灭，人们通宵守夜，等待辞旧迎新的时刻。守岁，象征着把一切邪瘟病疫照跑驱走，寓意期待新的一年吉祥如意。

除夕，在国人心中是具有特殊意义的，在这个年尾最重要的日子里，漂泊再远的游子也要赶着回家去和家人团聚，在爆竹声中辞旧岁，于烟花满天中迎新春。

Chapter 15
Chinese New Year's Eve

Chinese New Year's Eve, is the last night at the end of the lunar year. Chinese New Year's Eve is also called Danian Sanshi, because it is usually on the twenty-ninth or the thirtieth day of the twelfth lunar month. Chinese New Year's Eve is a time for getting rid of the old and introducing the new, family reunion and ancestor worship. Like the Qingming Festival, the Zhongyuan Festival and the Double Ninth Festival, Chinese New Year's Eve is also the traditional Chinese ancestor worship festival. Influenced by Chinese culture, Chinese New Year's Eve is also a traditional festival for countries in Chinese cultural sphere and overseas Chinese around the world.

Chinese New Year's Eve is the eve of the Spring Festival, also known as Nian Sanshi. There is a legend: in ancient times, there was a vicious monster called Xi, who came out to harm people at the end of each year. Later, people knew that the Xi was most afraid of the color of red and sound, so on the night of Nian Sanshi, every household pasted red couplets and set off firecrackers to drive away the Xi in order to seek peace in the New Year. This custom has been handed down since then, and the last night of one year is called "Chu Xi".

Song Dynasty is regarded as the peak period of ancient Chinese traditional culture by later generations. On the basis of inheriting the related customs of

Zhou, Qin, Han and Tang Dynasties, the Chinese New Year's Eve rituals and customs of Song Dynasty also have the change and innovation for keeping pace with the times. Before the Chinese New Year's Eve in the Song Dynasty, the sale of festival items, gifts giving (between sovereign and minister, and among relatives and friends), cleanliness and sanitation, pasting door gods, offering sacrifices to ancestors, setting off firecrackers and other Chinese New Year's Eve ritual activities have strong characteristics of the times.

Chinese New Year's Eve has been a tradition of worshipping ancestors, keeping the vigil until midnight, having reunion dinner, sticking New Year's Annual Red, hanging lanterns and so on since ancient times, which has been circulating for a long time. In many places people will choose the day of Chinese New Year's Eve for cleaning, when the Chinese New Year's Eve has passed and the Spring Festival started, people can no longer move the broom, as people believe that will drive away the good fortune. The most important thing on Chinese New Year's Eve is to paste red couplets. People buy red couplets, pictures of gods of wealth, window paper cuttings and so on, and paste them on doors and windows at home, which means that we will have happiness in the coming year. On Chinese New Year's Eve, the whole family has a "reunion dinner" together, with a family reunion flavor. After having reunion dinner on Chinese New Year's Eve, it's time to stay up. Keeping the vigil until midnight on Chinese New Year's Eve is one of the most important activities of the Chinese New Year's Eve with a long history. The folk custom of keeping the vigil until midnight is mainly manifested in the fact that the lights will not go out all night on Chinese New Year's Eve, waiting for the moment of leaving the old and welcoming the new throughout the whole night. It symbolizes driving away all evil plagues and epidemics, expressing the hope for a prosperous and auspicious New Year.

Chinese New Year's Eve is of special significance in the hearts of Chinese people. On this most important day at the end of year, wanderers who wander farther away are also rushing home to reunite with their families, saying goodbye to the old year in the sound of firecrackers, and greeting the new spring with fireworks all over the sky.

下篇　精神民俗文化

Part Ⅲ　Spiritual Folklore Culture

第一章　马街书会

马街书会，俗称"十三马街会"，是一场中国民间曲艺盛会。农历正月十三，全国数千名曲艺艺人会聚于河南省宝丰县的马街村，在火神庙旁举行祭拜师祖和收徒拜师仪式。40多种曲艺曲种和上千部传统及现代曲目在这里集中展现。2006年，马街书会被列入第一批国家级非物质文化遗产名录。

元朝延祐年间，马街书会初具规模，每年约有千名艺人前来说书。清代同治年间尤为兴盛，在同治二年（1863年），到会的艺人有2700人。马街书会被称为中国文化史上一大奇观，绵延700多年而不衰。

每年农历正月十三，来自河南各地及山东、河北、安徽、湖北、四川、江苏、陕西、甘肃、北京、天津、上海等地的成百上千名曲艺艺人，负鼓携琴，会集马街。马街书会无疑是众多艺人吹拉弹唱、表现自我、展示自我的民间文化盛会。其乐器种类之多、曲种曲目之繁杂，令人称奇。参演曲艺有河南坠子、湖北渔鼓、四川清音、山东琴书、凤阳花鼓、上海评话、徐州琴书、三弦书、大鼓书、评书、乱弹、道情等。

艺人在书会上说唱为"亮书"，邀请艺人说唱为"写书"。"亮书"是指艺人们在书会会场上摆阵对歌，以展示自己吹拉弹唱的技能。而"写书"一词并非指著书立传，它是随着中原文化的发展，自然形成的一种文化交流现象。在乡下如果家里"过事"❶，人们就会来到书会上选择说书人，他们以质论价，请说书人来家中演唱。书价是根据上年收成的好坏和艺人说唱水平的高低而定的。每年的马街书会都要评出"书会状元"，"书会状元"都是唱得最好的、书价最高的、最受群众欢迎的艺人。

马街书会具有独特的民间艺术表演魅力和浓厚的文化底蕴，它被誉为"中国十大民俗"之一，宝丰县也因此荣获"曲艺之乡"和"中国民间艺术之乡"的称号。

---

❶ "过事"是河南方言，意为办婚事。

Chapter 1
Majie Shu Hui

Majie Shu Hui, commonly known as the "Thirteen Majie Festival", is a grand Chinese folk Quyi festival. On the thirteenth day of the first lunar month, thousands of folk Quyi artists gathered in Majie Village, Baofeng County, Henan Province to worship ancestors of storytelling and accepting apprentices beside the Temple of Fire. More than 40 kinds of Quyi and thousands of traditional and modern repertoires are concentrated here. In 2006, it was included in the first batch of National Intangible Cultural Heritage List.

During the Yanyou period of the Yuan Dynasty, the Majie Shu Hui began to take shape, with about 1000 artists coming here to do storytelling every year, especially during the Tongzhi period of the Qing Dynasty. In the second year of Tongzhi (1863), 2700 artists attended the festival. Majie Shu Hui was called a great wonder in the history of Chinese culture, lasting for more than 700 years.

Every year, on the thirteenth day of the first lunar month, hundreds and thousands of Quyi artists from all parts of Henan, Shandong, Hebei, Anhui, Hubei, Sichuan, Jiangsu, Shaanxi, Gansu, Beijing, Tianjin and Shanghai gather on Majie with drums and Qins. The Majie Shu Hui is undoubtedly a grand folk cultural event for many artists to play and sing, to express and show themselves. It is amazing that there are so many kinds of musical instruments and so many kinds of music. There are Henan Zhuizi, Hubei Yugu, Sichuan Qingyin, Shandong Qinshu, Fengyang Huagu, Shanghai Pinghua, Xuzhou Qinshu, Sanxian Shu, Dagu Shu, Ping Shu, Luantan, Daoqing and so on.

Artists sing as "Liangshu" at the Shu Hui and invite artists to sing as "Xieshu". "Liangshu" refers to the artists set up formations and sing in antiphonal style at the venue of the Shu Hui to display their skills of playing and singing. The word "Xieshu" does not refer to writing a book to record someone's deeds. It is a natural phenomenon of cultural exchange with the development of Central Plains culture. In the countryside, if "Guoshi"[1] happened at home, people will come to the Shu Hui and choose the storyteller. They will discuss the price with quality and ask the storyteller to sing in the house. The price of the storytelling depends on the harvest last year and the level of artists' storytelling. Every year, the Majie Shu Hui will select the "Shu Hui Champion". The "Shu Hui Champion" is the best artist with the highest price, and is the most popular one.

Because of its unique charm of folk art performance and strong cultural heritage, Majie Shu Hui is known as one of the "Ten Folk Customs of China". Baofeng County is named "Town of Quyi" and "Town of Chinese Folk Art".

---

[1] "Guoshi" is a dialect in Henan, meaning to hold a wedding ceremony.

第二章　嵩山少林武术

　　嵩山少林寺，建于北魏孝文帝时期，是中国佛教禅宗祖庭和中国少林武术的发源地，现为世界文化遗产、全国重点文物保护单位、国家AAAAA级旅游景区。少林是中华武术中体系最庞大的门派，武术套路高达七百种以上，又因以禅入武、习武修禅，又有"武术禅"之称。

　　唐初，少林寺十三僧人因助李世民讨伐王世充有功，受到唐朝封赏，被特别准许设立常备僧兵，这成就了少林武术的发展。如今，少林寺因武艺高超享誉海内外，"少林"一词也成为中国传统武术的象征之一。

　　相传著名的达摩祖师在嵩山面壁修炼九年的漫长岁月中，创造了少林武术流派，这一传说使少林武术一开始就具备了深厚的人文文化内涵，最终形成了修身养性、善化人性、清净无为的武德。如今，少林武术作为一种人文文化现象，作为一种人体形态文化或是作为健身、御敌、竞技专案，在中国早已家喻户晓、妇孺皆知，已成为中华文化的宝贵遗产。

　　少林功夫内容丰富、套路繁多。按性质大致可分为内功、外功、硬功、轻功、气功等。内功以练精气为主；外功、硬功多指锻炼身体某一局部的猛力；轻功专练纵跳和超距；气功包括练气和养气。按技法又分拳术、棍术、枪术、刀术、剑术、技击散打、器械和器械对练等一百多种。

　　少林武术是中国武术最具代表性、最具文化内涵、最具宗教文化底蕴、最具完整体系、最具权威性、最具神秘感的流派，它无疑已成为中国武术的主流学派。

少林功夫作为中国功夫的典型代表，秉承"匡扶正义、除暴安良、追求和谐"的武术精神，并向大众传播博大精深的中原文化和中原人吃苦耐劳的精神。

Chapter 2
Songshan Shaolin Wushu

Songshan Shaolin Temple, built in the period of Emperor Xiaowen of the Northern Wei Dynasty, is the birthplace of Buddhism's Chan Sect (Zen) in China as well as the cradle of China's Shaolin Wushu (martial arts). It is now a world cultural heritage, a national key cultural relics protection unit, and a national AAAAA-level tourist attraction. Shaolin is the largest school in Chinese Wushu system. There are more than 700 kinds of Wushu routines. It is also known as "Wushu Zen" because it integrates Zen into Wushu practice, and through Wushu, one cultivates Zen.

At the beginning of Tang Dynasty, the thirteen monks of Shaolin Temple were awarded a prize by the Tang Dynasty because they helped Li Shimin to fight against Wang Shichong. They were specially allowed to establish standing monk soldiers, which achieves the development of Shaolin Wushu. Shaolin Temple is renowned at home and abroad for its excellent martial arts. The word "Shaolin" has also become one of the symbols of Chinese traditional martial arts.

Legend has it that the famous Bodhidharma created the Shaolin Wushu school in the long years (9 years) of cultivation facing the wall in Songshan, and made Shaolin Wushu possess profound humanistic and cultural connotations from the beginning, with martial virtue of self-cultivation, refining human nature, Quietism and Non-Action. As a cultural phenomenon, Shaolin Wushu has become a precious heritage of Chinese culture as a human body shape culture or as a fitness, enemy defense and competitive project, which has been well known to all households, even to women and children in China.

Shaolin Kungfu is rich in content with various routines. According to its nature, it can be roughly divided into internal Gong ("Gong" means a kind of skill in Chinese), external Gong, hard Gong, lightness Gong, Qi Gong and so on. Internal Gong mainly focuses on practicing essence; external and hard Gong mostly refer to exercising a part of the body's strength; lightness Gong specializes in vertical jump and over-distance; Qi Gong includes practicing Qi and nourishing Qi. According to techniques, there are more than 100 kinds, such as boxing, staff skills, spear skills, broadsword skills, sword skills, Sanda, martial arts weapon, armed combat and so on.

Shaolin Wushu is also the most representative, the most cultural, the most religious, the most complete, the most authoritative and the most mysterious school of Chinese Wushu. It has undoubtedly become the mainstream school of Chinese Wushu.

Shaolin Kungfu is a typical representative of Chinese Kungfu. Its theme is "upholding justice, getting rid of the cruel and pacifying the good people, pursuing harmony", and disseminates to the public the profound culture of the Central Plains, as well as the spirit of the people of the Central Plains to bear hardships and endure hard work.

第三章　陈家沟太极拳

陈家沟太极拳是太极拳的一个重要的分支和流派。陈氏一族流传的太极拳，传到后世分为许多支派，为了便于与其他各派太极拳有所区别，所以称为"陈家太极拳"，有时也称为"陈氏""陈派"或"陈式"。目前"陈式太极拳"已经成为河南的一个著名文化品牌，2006年被列为第一批国家级非物质文化遗产。

陈氏一族是在明洪武七年（1374年）在族长陈卜率领下由山西洪洞县大槐树村移居到河南温县常阳村，移居后即以陈卜为第一代。后来，家族繁衍，遂把此地改名为"陈家沟"。移居到河南的陈姓一族，为了防匪自卫，全族很早就练武。传至第十四代陈长兴（1771—1853）时，陈式太极拳已趋精简定型。

陈式太极拳采取阴阳学说，以动静开合之理，与刚柔虚实之法，为轻沉迟速互练之术；拳势动作，均以螺旋进退，称缠丝劲，为陈氏独创之奥秘，世代口口相传；于技击则有以小力胜大力、弱慢胜强快的效果。

陈氏世代相传之太极拳，原有七套。为长拳一套，十三势头一套，二套、三套、四套、五套，及炮捶一套。传至陈氏第十四世陈长兴、陈有本时，陈氏太极拳由博而约，专练十三势头套及炮捶两套。因此现今陈氏传授之太极拳仅为两套：十三势老架、炮捶。陈氏太极拳实为我国武术中极为上乘、高深、奥妙的拳法。

河南温县陈家沟村的太极拳，是一种独特的集技击、健身和养生功能为一体的民间体育活动，至今已有 400 多年的历史。它深受全世界人民的青睐，每年都有来自不同国家和地区的数以万计的太极拳爱好者前往陈家沟学习太极拳。

Chapter 3
Chenjiagou Tai Chi

Chen Jiagou Tai Chi is an important branch and school of Tai Chi. Tai Chi handed down by Chen clan can be divided into many branches in later generations. In order to distinguish Tai Chi from other schools, it is called "Chen Jia Tai Chi", sometimes also called "Chen Clan" "Chen Faction" or "Chen Style". At present, "Chen Style Tai Chi" has become a famous cultural brand in Henan Province, and was included in the first batch of National Intangible Cultural Heritage in 2006.

In the seventh year of Hongwu in Ming Dynasty (1374), Chen family migrated from Dahuaishu Village in Hongtong County of Shanxi Province to Changyang Village in Wen County of Henan Province under the leadership of Chen Bu, the leader of Chen clan. After immigration, Chen Bu was the first generation. Later, the family multiplied and renamed the place as "Chen Jiagou". The Chen family, who emigrated to Henan Province, practiced martial arts very early in order to defend themselves against bandits. By the time it reached the fourteenth generation, represented by Chen Changxing, Chen Style Tai Chi had become refined and standardized.

Chen Style Tai Chi adopts the theory of Yin and Yang, using the principles of movement and stillness, opening and closing, as well as the methods of hardness and softness, virtuality and reality, as a technique for mutually practicing lightness and heaviness, slowness and speed. The movements of boxing are all spiral forward and backward, which is called the spiral strength, and the mystery of Chen's original creation, which is handed down from generation to generation. While in fighting, it has the effect of winning large strength with small strength and overcoming strong speed with weak slowness.

There are seven sets of Tai Chi handed down from generation to generation by Chen's family. One set of Changquan, one set of thirteen postures, two, three, four, five sets, and one set of Pao Chui (Cannon Fist). When it was spread to Chen Changxing and Chen Youben, the fourteenth generation of the Chen's family, Chen's Tai Chi, from the broad to the simple, specializing in thirteen postures and two sets of Pao Chui. As a result, Chen's Tai Chi is taught only two sets nowadays: thirteen postures and Pao Chui. It is indeed the most excellent, profound and mysterious boxing method in Chinese martial arts.

Tai Chi of Chenjiagou Village, Wen County, Henan Province, is a unique folk sport with the functions of fighting, fitness and health preservation. It has a history of more than 400 years. It is well received by people all over the world. Every year tens of thousands of Tai Chi fans from different countries and regions of the world come to Chenjiagou to study Tai Chi.

第四章　洛阳牡丹文化节

　　洛阳牡丹文化节，前身为河南省洛阳牡丹花会，是全国四大名会之一，2008 年入选国家非物质文化遗产名录。1983 年至 2024 年，洛阳已连续成功举办了 41 届牡丹花会。自 2010 年起，河南省洛阳牡丹花会正式升格为中国洛阳牡丹文化节。

　　中原气候温和、阳光充足，自唐以来，洛阳牡丹便有了"甲天下"的美誉。唐朝就有"花开花落二十日，一城之人皆若狂"的观花习俗。每到春暖花开的季节，牡丹竞相开放，花团锦簇、美不胜收。

　　洛阳牡丹是毛茛科、芍药属植物，为多年生落叶灌木，中文别名为鹿韭、木芍药、富贵花等。洛阳牡丹花朵硕大、品种繁多，主要有红、白、粉、黄、紫、蓝、绿、黑及复色 9 大色系，10 种花型，1000 多个品种。洛阳牡丹是中国特有的木本名贵花卉，有数千年的自然生长历史和 1500 多年的人工栽培历史。其在中国栽培甚广，并早已引种世界各地。在中国，牡丹花被拥戴为花中之王，相关文化和绘画作品很丰富。

　　在中国传统文化中，牡丹雍容华贵、端庄富丽的形象引发人们诸多联想，派生出与之相关联的文化象征意义，并形成牡丹文化的基本内涵。自唐宋以来，牡丹成为吉祥幸福、繁荣昌盛的象征，并得以世代延续下来。在人民群众的心目中，牡丹是美的化身，是吉祥与富贵的象征。国尊繁荣昌盛，家重富贵平安，人喜幸福吉祥，这些特点和寓意，牡丹兼而有之。

中国洛阳牡丹文化节是一个融赏花观灯、旅游观光、经贸合作与交流为一体的大型综合性经济文化活动，已经成为洛阳人民政治、经济、文化生活中的一件大事，是洛阳人民不可或缺的盛大节日，是洛阳发展经济的平台和展示城市形象的窗口，更是洛阳走向世界的桥梁和世界了解洛阳的名片。

Chapter 4
The Peony Culture Festival of Luoyang

The Peony Culture Festival of Luoyang, formerly Luoyang Peony Flower Fair in Henan Province, one of the four great national festivals, has been selected into the National Intangible Cultural Heritage List in 2008. From 1983 to 2024, Luoyang has successfully held peony fair for 41 times. Since 2010, Luoyang Peony Flower Fair in Henan Province has been upgraded to the Peony Culture Festival of Luoyang in China.

Since the Tang Dynasty, Luoyang peony has gained the reputation of "the first one under heaven" with mild climate and abundant sunshine in the Central Plains. In the Tang Dynasty, there was the custom of "flowers blossom and fall in twenty days, and people in city are all crazy". Every spring season, peony blossoms in glorious profusion, presenting a scene of indescribable beauty.

Luoyang peony is a perennial deciduous shrub belonging to Ranunculaceae family and Paeonia genus. Its common Chinese names include Lujiu, Mushaoyao, Fuguihua and so on. Luoyang peony has large flowers and a wide variety of breeds. There are 9 major color series, including red, white, pink, yellow, purple, blue, green, black and polychrome, and 10 flower types and more than 1000 varieties. Luoyang peony is a unique woody precious flower in China. It has thousands of years of natural growth history and more than 1500 years of artificial cultivation history. It is widely cultivated in China and has been introduced all over the world. Peony flowers are embraced as the king of flowers in China, rich in cultural and painting works.

In Chinese traditional culture, peony is elegant, dignified and magnificent, which arouses many associations, derives the cultural symbolic meaning associated with it, and forms the basic connotation of peony culture. Since the Tang and Song Dynasties, peony has become a symbol of auspiciousness, happiness and prosperity, and has been passed down for generations. In the minds of the people, peony is the embodiment of beauty, the symbol of good fortune and wealth. The nation is respected for its prosperity and strength; the family values wealth, peace and well-being; and people like happiness and auspiciousness. Peony has all these characteristics and implications.

The Chinese Luoyang Peony Culture Festival is a large-scale comprehensive economic and cultural activity which combines enjoying flower and lantern, tourism, economic and trade cooperation and exchange. It has become a major event in the political, economic and cultural life of Luoyang people. It is an indispensable grand festival for the people of Luoyang, a platform for Luoyang's economic development and a window for displaying the image of the city, a bridge for Luoyang to enter the world and a name card that lets the world know about Luoyang.

第五章　开封菊花文化节

中国开封菊花文化节前身为中国开封菊花花会，始于 1983 年，2013 年升格为国家级节会，更名为"中国开封菊花文化节"。中国开封菊花文化节是一个融赏花观灯、旅游观光、经贸合作与交流为一体的大型综合性经济文化活动。

1983 年，开封市第七届人大常委会第十七次会议确定"菊花"为开封市市花，并确定每年 10 月至 11 月举办"中国开封菊花花会"。从 1983 年到 2013 年，中国开封菊花花会经历了规模由小到大、档次由低到高的发展历程。2013 年"中国开封菊花花会"升格为"中国开封菊花文化节"。

中国开封菊花文化节举办时间在 10 至 11 月间。主要展区位于万岁山大宋武侠城、龙亭公园、清明上河园、铁塔公园、天波杨府、翰园碑林、禹王台公园。

中国开封菊花文化节的吉祥物结合了中国传统福娃造型，塑造出活泼可爱的"菊娃""菊妮"形象，展现"菊城宋都"开封灿烂的历史和"大宋菊花"的文化内涵。吉祥物整体表现朱仙镇年画名作"招财童子"元素，体现出开封历史文化源远流长，表达出热忱欢迎四海宾朋欢聚（菊）开封、赏花做客的开放态度。

中国开封菊花文化节作为我国节庆活动中的知名品牌，在扩大开放与交流、推动开封经济振兴、促进文化旅游产业发展、提升城市形象和品位等方面发挥着无可替代的作用。

Chapter 5
The Chrysanthemum Culture Festival
of Kaifeng

Chrysanthemum Culture Festival of Kaifeng in China, formerly known as China Kaifeng Chrysanthemum Flower Fair, began in 1983 and was upgraded to a national festival in 2013, renamed "Chrysanthemum Culture Festival of Kaifeng in China". Chrysanthemum Culture Festival of Kaifeng in China is a large-scale comprehensive economic and cultural activity which integrates enjoying flower and lantern, tourism, economic and trade cooperation and exchanges.

In 1983, the 17th meeting of the Standing Committee of the Seventh Municipal People's Congress decided on "Chrysanthemum" as the city flower of Kaifeng, and decided to hold "China Kaifeng Chrysanthemum Flower Fair" from October to November every year. From 1983 to 2013, China Kaifeng Chrysanthemum Flower Fair has experienced a development process from small to large scale and from low to high level. In 2013, "China Kaifeng Chrysanthemum Flower Fair" was renamed "Chrysanthemum Culture Festival of Kaifeng in China".

The Chrysanthemum Culture Festival of Kaifeng in China is held between

October to November. The main exhibition areas are located in Wansuishan Dasong Wuxia Theme Park, Longting Park, Qingming Shanghe Garden, Iron Tower Park, Tianbo Yangfu, Hanyuan Stele Forest and Yuwangtai Park.

The mascot of the Chrysanthemum Culture Festival of Kaifeng in China combines traditional Chinese Fuwa sculpture to create lively and lovely "Juwa" and "Juni" images, showing the brilliant history of "Chrysanthemum City and Song Dynasty's Capital" Kaifeng and the cultural connotation of "Dasong Chrysanthemum". The whole mascot embodies the elements of Zhuxian Town's famous New Year's Painting "Fortune-Bringing Child", which reflects the long history and culture of Kaifeng, and expresses the open attitude of warmly welcoming friends from all over the world to gather (with same pronunciation as chrysanthemum in Chinese) in Kaifeng and enjoy the flowers and be guests.

Chrysanthemum Culture Festival of Kaifeng in China, as a famous brand in festival activities in China, plays an irreplaceable role in expanding opening-up and communication, promoting Kaifeng's economic revitalization, advancing the development of cultural tourism industry, and enhancing the image and taste of the city.

第六章　朱仙镇木版年画

朱仙镇木版年画历史悠久、风格独特，是全国著名的年画之一，也是中国古老的传统工艺品之一。作为中国木版年画的鼻祖，它主要分布于河南省开封市朱仙镇及其周边地区。朱仙镇木版年画构图饱满，线条粗犷简练，造型古朴夸张，色彩新鲜艳丽。2006 年，朱仙镇木版年画被列入第一批国家级非物质文化遗产名录。

朱仙镇木版年画诞生于唐，兴于宋，鼎盛于明。北宋初年，宋都东京是全国政治、经济、文化的中心，故该地木版年画的发展成为历史必然。北宋末期，由于金兵的入侵，东京的木版年画业迁至东京 45 里外的朱仙镇。明清时期，朱仙镇成为中原的商业重镇，木版年画在繁荣的商埠迅速恢复。抗日战争爆发前，朱仙镇木版年画业迁往开封，自此又掀起木版年画繁荣的第三次高潮。

朱仙镇木版年画来自民间、流传于民间，经历代手工艺人之手而融入了民族传统文化的审美观念和崇神意识。年画中画得最多的就是门神，门神中以秦琼、尉迟恭两位武将为主。除此之外，还有各种文、武门神。

朱仙镇木版年画制作采用木版与镂版相结合，水印套色，种类繁多，用纸讲究，色彩艳丽，庄重深厚。其刀技线条粗犷豪放，阴粗阳细，阴阳对比性较强。同时，朱仙镇木版年画十分讲究用色，其所用颜料以矿物、植物作为原料，自行手工磨制而成，磨出的颜料色彩十分纯净，使印制的年画明快鲜艳、久不褪色。朱仙镇木版年画展现出中华民族的用色审美，即崇尚使用暖色，如丹红、木红、桃红、槐黄、桔黄等，显得热烈奔放。

朱仙镇木版年画，不但具有极高的艺术收藏价值，而且极具观赏价值。开封已挖掘、整理出的年画老版有二百二十余块，重新印制历史老版年画三百多套，为保护本地传统木版年画做了大量有益的工作。朱仙镇镇政府也加大了对人才的培养和对老艺人的保护，以促进朱仙镇木版年画的传承和发展。

Chapter 6
The Woodblock New Year Paintings of Zhuxian Town

The Woodblock New Year Paintings of Zhuxian Town have a long history and unique style. They are one of the famous New Year Paintings in China and also one of the ancient Chinese traditional crafts. As the originator of Chinese Woodblock New Year Paintings, they are mainly distributed in Zhuxian Town, Kaifeng, and its surrounding areas in Henan Province. The Woodblock New Year Paintings of Zhuxian Town have full composition, rough and concise lines, simple and exaggerated shapes, and fresh and brilliant colors. In 2006, it was included in the first batch of National Intangible Cultural Heritage List.

The Woodblock New Year Paintings of Zhuxian Town were born in the Tang Dynasty, advanced in the Song Dynasty and flourished in the Ming Dynasty. In the early Northern Song Dynasty, Dongjing, the capital of the Song Dynasty, was the political, economic and cultural center of the country, making the development of Woodblock New Year Paintings inevitable. In the late Northern Song Dynasty, due to the invasion of the Jin army, the Woodblock New Year Paintings industry in Dongjing moved to Zhuxian Town, 45 Li (Li was an ancient Chinese unit of measurement. In Song Dynasty, 1 Li was approximately equal to 454.2 meters.) away from Dongjing. During the Ming and Qing Dynasties, Zhuxian Town became a major commercial town in the Central Plains, and Woodblock New Year Paintings quickly recovered in prosperous commercial ports. Before the outbreak of the War of Resistance Against Japanese Aggression, Zhuxian Town's Woodblock New Year Paintings industry moved to Kaifeng. Since then, the third climax of the prosperity of Woodblock New Year Paintings has been set off.

The Woodblock New Year Paintings of Zhuxian Town come from the folk and spread among the people. Through the hands of craftsmen for generations, they have integrated the aesthetic concept and god-worship consciousness of the traditional national culture. The Door Gods are the most frequently painted in the New Year's Paintings, in which Qin Qiong and Yuchi Gong are the two main military generals. In addition, there are all kinds of literary and martial (wenwu in Chinese) Door Gods.

Zhuxian Town Woodblock New Year Paintings are made by combining woodblock with engraving. It adopts the technique of watermark overprinting, with a wide variety of types. Great attention is paid to the choice of paper, and the colors are bright and gorgeous, presenting a solemn and profound style. Zhuxian Town Woodblock New Year Paintings carving technique and line is rough and bold, with thick Yinke (carved in intaglio) and thin Yangke (carved in relief), the contrast between Yinke and Yangke is strong. Zhuxian Town Woodblock New Year Paintings are very particular about color, the pigments used are self-grinded by hands using minerals and plants as raw materials, the color of the ground pigments is very pure, and the printed New Year Paintings are bright and lively, and do not fade for a long time. Zhuxian Town Woodblock

New Year Paintings show the color aesthetics of the Chinese nation. It advocates the use of warm colors, such as bright red, wood red, peach red, sophora yellow, orange yellow, and so on, appears to be bold and unrestrained.

The Woodblock New Year Paintings of Zhuxian Town are not only of great artistic collection value, but also of great ornamental value. There have excavated and sorted out more than 220 planks of old prints of New Year Paintings, reprinting more than 300 sets of historical old prints in Kaifeng, which has done a lot of useful work for the protection of local traditional Woodblock New Year Paintings. The Zhuxian Town Government has increased the training of talents and the protection of old artists, aiming to promote the inheritance and development of Woodblock New Year Paintings of Zhuxian Town.

第七章　开封斗鸡

　　中原斗鸡是"中国四大斗鸡"之一，而中原一带的斗鸡，追根溯源，大多出自开封斗鸡。开封斗鸡是"国宝级名鸡"，已经被列入了国家地方品种保护名录。开封斗鸡活动也是一种历史悠久的娱乐活动。从北宋至近代，开封斗鸡活动一直盛行于民间。

　　开封在唐朝受重视程度仅次于当时的长安和洛阳。开封百业俱兴，各方面都发展得很好，斗鸡也在唐朝发展到鼎盛状态。当北宋定都开封，斗鸡文化的中心也跟随权力中心的转移，从长安、洛阳等地转移到了开封。北宋以来，开封的斗鸡活动一直很盛行，并且遍及民间，斗鸡品种逐渐形成了不同的血统体系，玩斗鸡者也逐渐形成了不同的帮派系统。

　　要开展斗鸡比赛，需要确定比赛时间和比赛地点。开封斗鸡比赛固定在每年农历正月初二举行。除了正月初二外，二、三、四月的比赛时间都不固定，一般都选在月初第一个星期日。比赛地点即斗鸡坑，因斗鸡的场地低于四周地面而得名，从清末到民国一直设在开封北部"里城"东门以外的广场上。现在，开封的"斗鸡坑"多选择在龙亭公园、铁塔公园和相国寺内。

　　开封的斗鸡爱好者，当地俗称"玩斗鸡"。他们多爱练武，又爱喝酒，义气深重，纪律严明。玩斗鸡的人都有一种传统，即"论道不论亲"，如果有人真正爱鸡，通过朋友介绍，都可无偿赠送斗鸡，但是必须遵守帮规：斗鸡只能自养不能转让，更不能与其他鸡交配繁殖。

旧时斗鸡是一种赌博。现在，斗鸡逐渐成为深受广大开封市民喜爱的体育休闲运动，玩斗鸡不仅锻炼了身体，也陶冶了情操。斗鸡比赛丰富了开封市民的业余文化生活。

Chapter 7
Cockfighting in Kaifeng

Central Plains' fighting cock is one of "China's four famous fighting cocks". Most of the fighting cocks in Central Plains originated from Kaifeng fighting cocks. Kaifeng fighting cock is a famous national treasure cock, which has been listed in the National List of Local Varieties Protection. Kaifeng cockfighting is also a kind of entertainment with long history. From the Northern Song Dynasty to modern times, cockfighting in Kaifeng has been popular among the people.

Kaifeng was was highly valued, only second to Chang'an and Luoyang in the Tang Dynasty. Kaifeng was thriving in all walks of life, and all aspects of development were very good. Cockfighting in Kaifeng developed to its peak in the Tang Dynasty. When Kaifeng became the capital of the Northern Song Dynasty, the cockfighting center also followed the transfer of power center changing from Chang'an, Luoyang and other places to Kaifeng. Since the Northern Song Dynasty, cockfighting activities in Kaifeng have been very popular, and spread throughout the folklore. Cock breeds have gradually formed different lineage systems, and cock fighters have gradually formed different clique systems.

To hold a cockfighting competition, it is necessary to determine the competition time and location. The cockfighting competition in Kaifeng is fixed to be held on the second day of the first lunar month every year. Except for the second day of the first lunar month, the matches in Lunar February, March and April are not fixed, usually on the first Sunday of the beginning of month. The competition venue is cockfighting pit, which is named because the cockfighting ground is lower than the surrounding ground. From the end of Qing Dynasty to the Republic of China, Kaifeng's "cockfighting pit" has been on the square outside the east gate of "Licheng" in the north of Kaifeng. Now, more Kaifeng's "cockfighting pit" are made in Longting Park, Iron Tower Park and Xiangguo Temple.

Kaifeng cockfighting enthusiasts, commonly known locally as "playing cockfighting", who are fond of practicing martial arts and drinking. They have a deep sense of righteousness and strict discipline. People who play cockfighting have a tradition of "talking about Tao regardless of relatives". If someone really loves fighting cocks, they can give them free through friends' introduction, but they must abide by the rules: fighting cock can only be self-raised and can not be transferred, let alone copulated with other chickens.

In the old days, cockfighting was a kind of gambling. Now, cockfighting has gradually become a popular and leisure sport among the Kaifeng general public. Playing cockfighting not only exercises the body, but also cultivates the sentiment. The cockfighting competition enlivens the amateur cultural life of the Kaifeng citizens.

第八章　豫剧

　　豫剧起源于中原，是中国五大戏曲剧种之一、中国第一大地方剧种，也是在中国具有广泛影响力的戏曲剧种。豫剧以唱功见长，唱腔流畅、节奏鲜明、吐字清晰，行腔酣畅淋漓、大开大合，音乐丰富多彩，表演风格朴实，富有浓厚的乡土气息，观众人数在全国所有剧种中最多。

　　豫剧，又称"河南梆子"。一说由明代末期传入河南的山陕梆子结合河南土语及民间曲调发展而成，现流行于河南、河北、山西、山东等省份。原有豫东调、豫西调、祥符调、沙河调四大派别，现以豫东调、豫西调为主。出现过常香玉、陈素真、崔兰田、马金凤、阎立品等著名旦角演员。剧目有《穆桂英挂帅》《红娘》《花打朝》《对花枪》和现代戏《朝阳沟》等。

　　在发展过程中，豫剧也形成了独特的个人流派，这些流派对豫剧的改革和发展起到了巨大的推动作用。豫剧旦角流派有：悠长天籁的"陈派"（创始人陈素真），高亢激昂的"常派"（创始人常香玉），韵味醇厚的"崔派"（创始人崔兰田），大气响亮的"马派"（创始人马金凤），委婉含蓄的"阎派"（创始人阎立品），缠绵委婉的"桑派"（创始人桑振君）。豫剧生行流派有：豫东调"唐派"（创始人唐玉成），祥符、沙河调"唐派"（创始人唐喜成）。豫剧净行流派：豫剧"李派"（创始人李斯忠）。豫剧丑角流派：豫剧"牛派"（创始人牛得草）。

    1994 年，河南卫视推出《梨园春》栏目，推动了豫剧在全国及全世界的发展和繁荣，对弘扬中原民俗文化起到了积极的促进作用。

    豫剧是我国宝贵的戏剧艺术文化，经过众多豫剧艺术家的努力才使豫剧流传至今，并且得到大众的喜爱。豫剧文化可以说是中原民俗文化的代表，具有深厚的中原民俗文化特色。中原民俗文化催化豫剧艺术文化的产生，豫剧文化对于中原民俗文化也产生了积极的影响。

Chapter 8
Yu Opera

Yu Opera originated in the Central Plains, is one of the five major Chinese operas, the largest local opera in China, and also has a wide influence in China. Yu Opera is characterized by its excellent singing skills, smooth singing style, clear rhythm, clear pronunciation, fluent and incisive lines, wide opening and closing, rich and colorful music, simple performing style and strong local flavor. The audience is the largest in all kinds of operas in China.

Yu Opera, also known as Henan Bangzi. One view is that, in the late Ming Dynasty, Bangzi from Shanxi and Shaanxi, introduced to Henan Province, developed in combination with local dialects and folk tunes of Henan Province, is now popular in Henan, Hebei, Shanxi and Shandong provinces. Originally, there were four major schools of Eastern Henan Tune, Western Henan Tune, Xiangfu Tune and Shahe Tune, and now they are mainly based on Eastern Henan Tune and Western Henan Tune. Chang Xiangyu, Chen Suzhen, Cui Lantian, Ma Jinfeng, Yan Lipin and other famous Danjue actors (female roles) have appeared. The repertoires include *Lady General Mu Guiying Takes Command*, *Hongniang*, *Huadachao*, *Duel with Ornamented Spears* and Modern Drama *Chaoyanggou*.

In the process of development, Yu Opera has also formed a unique personal school, which has played a huge role in promoting the reform and development of Yu Opera. There are the following schools of Danjue in Yu Opera: The "Chen School" with its long and heavenly melodies was founded by Chen Suzhen. The "Chang School" featuring high-pitched and impassioned tunes was founded by Chang Xiangyu. The "Cui School" with its rich and mellow flavor was founded by Cui Lantian. The "Ma School" known for its grand and resounding style was founded by Ma Jinfeng. The "Yan School" with its gentle and implicit characteristics was founded by Yan Lipin. And the "Sang School" which is tender and euphemistic was founded by Sang Zhenjun. As for the schools of the Shenghang (male roles) in Yu Opera, the "Tang School" of the Yudong Tune was founded by Tang Yucheng, and the "Tang School" of the Xiangfu Tune and Shahe Tune was founded by Tang Xicheng. Regarding the schools of the Jinghang ("painted face" roles) in Yu Opera, the "Li School" was founded by Li Sizhong. When it comes to the schools of the Choujue (clowns) in Yu Opera, the "Niu School" was founded by Niu Decao.

In 1994, Henan Satellite TV launched the column *Liyuanchun*, which promoted the development and prosperity of Yu Opera in the whole country and the world, and played a positive role in promoting the Central Plains culture.

Yu Opera is a precious drama art and culture in our country. Through the efforts of many artists of Yu Opera, Yu Opera can be spread to the present day and is loved by many people. Yu Opera culture is the representative of the Central Plains folk culture, with profound characteristics of the Central Plains folk culture. The folk culture of the Central Plains catalyzed the emergence of the artistic culture of Yu Opera. Yu Opera culture also had a certain impact on the folk culture of the Central Plains.

第九章　洛阳唐三彩

唐三彩，中国古代陶瓷烧制工艺的珍品，全名唐代三彩釉陶器，是盛行于唐代的一种低温釉陶器，釉彩有黄、绿、白、褐、蓝等，以黄、绿、白三色为主，所以人们习惯称之为"唐三彩"。因唐三彩最早、最多出土于洛阳，亦有"洛阳唐三彩"之称，并且沿用至今，享誉中外。

唐三彩，最初是从唐墓挖掘出来的陶器之泛称，后被用作陶瓷分类的术语，并非专指三种色彩的唐代釉陶瓷。因为挖掘出来的各类陶俑、陶像及其他陶器上，有的只有单彩，或者二彩，也有的具有较复杂的多彩颜色。一般而言，除了胎体的白地之外，铅黄、绿、青三彩最为普遍，在三彩的调配技法上，也最富艺术的韵味。

唐三彩的品种很多，有立体塑像、有明器、也有生活用具。从现存的各种唐三彩看，它最完整地反映了唐代社会生活中的手工艺品种类，几乎没有一种材质的唐代手工艺品出土的种类可以超过唐三彩。

唐代"贞观之治"以后，国力强盛、百业俱兴，同时也导致了一些高官生活的腐化，于是厚葬之风日盛。当时唐三彩作为一种冥器，主要是为了模拟墓葬主人生前的生活场景，以供死者死后也能享受生前的荣华富贵。唐三彩的造型丰富多彩，一般分为动物、生活用具和人物三大类，其中尤以动物为多。

随着唐王朝的灭亡，唐三彩也随之消失。唐代以后，唐三彩的制作工艺在北方地区流传繁衍，其中包括契丹民族的三彩和北宋的宋三彩，还有金代的金三彩等。但它们的艺术水平与唐三彩相比较为逊色，风格也有较大的区别。

唐三彩集中体现了唐代的经济文化，在洛阳一地传承了千余年，是中国传统文化的瑰宝之一。随着人们对唐三彩的关注增多，以及唐三彩复原工艺的发展，人们热衷于将唐三彩作为文房陈设，唐三彩也成了馈赠亲友的佳品。

Chapter 9
Luoyang Tang Sancai

Tang Sancai, a treasure of ancient Chinese ceramic firing technigues, with full name of Tang-Dynasty-Tri-Color Glazed Pottery, is a low-temperature glazed pottery popular in the Tang Dynasty. The glaze has yellow, green, white, brown, blue and other colors, because of the three main colors of yellow, green and white, so people are accustomed to calling it "Tang Tri-Color". As the earliest unearthed and largest quantity in Luoyang, the Tang Sancai is also known as "Luoyang Tang Sancai", and has been used up to now, enjoying a good reputation both at home and abroad.

Tang Sancai was initially a generic term for pottery excavated from Tang tombs. Later, it was adopted as a term for ceramic classification and didn't specifically refer to the glazed pottery of the Tang Dynasty with just those three colors. Among the various pottery figurines, pottery statues and other pottery excavated, there are single-color or two-color pottery objects, while others have more complex and multiple colors. Generally speaking, besides the white ground of the body, the three colors of lead yellow, green and blue are the most common, and the three colors are also the most artistic in their blending techniques.

There are many kinds of Tang Sancai, such as three-dimensional statues, funerary utensils and living utensils. From the existing variety of Tang Sancai, it reflects the most complete kinds of handicraft of Tang Dynasty social life, almost no one of the Tang Dynasty handicraft made of any material can surpass the variety of Tang Sancai.

After the "Reign of Zhenguan" in Tang Dynasty, the country was strong and prosperous, all industries are thriving which also led to the corruption of the lives of some senior officials, so the wind of grand burial became more and more popular. At that time, Tang Sancai was used as a kind of funerary implements, mainly to simulate the life scene of the tomb owner and to provide the deceased with the glory and wealth of life after death. The diverse shapes of Tang Sancai are generally divided into three categories: animals, living utensils and characters, of which most are animals.

With the downfall of Tang Dynasty, the Tang Sancai also disappeared. After the Tang Dynasty, the production technology of Tang Sancai spread and multiplied in the northern region, including Sancai of the Khitan nationality and Song Sancai in the Northern Song Dynasty, and Jin Sancai in the Jin Dynasty. But their artistic level is inferior to that of Tang Sancai, and their styles are quite different.

The Tang Sancai embodies the economy and culture of Tang Dynasty. It has been inherited in Luoyang for more than a thousand years and is one of the treasures of Chinese traditional culture. With the increasing attention to the Tang Sancai and the development of the restoration technology of the Tang Sancai, people have been keen on using Tang Sancai as the display of the study, which is also a good gift for relatives and friends.

第十章　南阳玉雕

南阳玉，又称"独山玉"或"南玉"，产于河南省南阳市城区北边的独山，为中国四大名玉之一。南阳玉的开采和使用可追溯到 5000 多年前的新石器时代，在中国玉文化发展史上占有极其重要的地位。南阳玉雕在国际上亦享有盛誉，每年"五一"期间南阳都会举办"中国南阳玉雕节暨国际玉文化博览会"。

5000 年前的新石器时代，南阳勤劳智慧的先民就开始利用和雕琢独山玉了，当地玉文化开始出现萌芽并初步繁荣起来。到了汉代，南阳玉已被大量开采并雕琢，盛况可观，有了加工、雕刻玉器的聚居区。唐宋以后，南阳玉雕逐步由原来单纯作为进贡工艺品供达官贵人观赏享用，发展成为既有装饰品，又有生活使用器皿。明清时期，南阳玉雕品种已十分丰富。清代以后，南阳玉雕已形成一大行业。改革开放以来，久负盛名的南阳玉雕吸引了大量的业内外人士，从而使独山玉为更多的人所了解、欣赏和接受。

独山玉质地坚韧微密、细腻柔润，光泽透明，色泽斑驳陆离。有绿、白、黄、紫、红、黑 6 种色素 77 个色彩类型，是玉雕的一等原料。雕刻按技法不同分花活、素活两类，花活如花熏、转炉、飞禽、走兽、仕女人物等；素活如戒指、手镯、耳环等。独山玉雕成品晶莹闪烁、玲珑剔透，为南阳著名特产。

　　历经千年兴盛而不衰的玉雕产业，形成了传承悠久、积淀深厚的南阳玉文化，孕育了一代又一代、代代相传、层出不穷、技艺高超的南阳玉雕艺人。南阳的玉雕艺术大师们在继承传统工艺的同时，不断引进、吸收、创新艺术设计和雕刻手法。正是悠久的历史、深厚的文化底蕴和得天独厚的美玉资源相结合，才使得南阳玉雕这一艺术瑰宝得以发扬光大。

Chapter 10
Nanyang Jade Carving

Nanyang Jade, also known as "Dushan Jade" or "Nan Jade", is produced in Dushan, north of Nanyang City, Henan Province. It is one of the four famous jades in China. The mining and utilization of Nanyang Jade began in the Neolithic Age more than five thousand years ago and occupies an extremely important position in the history of the development of Chinese Jade Culture. Nanyang Jade Carving also enjoys a high reputation in the world. Every year during May Day Holiday, Nanyang hosts "the Nanyang Jade Carving Festival of China and the International Jade Culture Exposition".

In the Neolithic Age more than five thousand years ago, the industrious and wise ancestors in Nanyang began to use and carve the Dushan jade, and the jade culture began to germinate and flourish initially. By the Han Dynasty, Nanyang Jade had been exploited and carved in large quantities. It had a magnificent and grand occasion, with a settlement of processing and carving jade articles. After the Tang and Song Dynasties, Nanyang Jade Carving gradually developed from mere as a tribute for nobles and officials to both decorations and living utensils. The variety of Nanyang Jade Carvings in Ming and Qing Dynasties was very rich. After the Qing Dynasty, Nanyang Jade Carving has formed a major industry. Since the reform and opening-up, the well-known Nanyang Jade

Carving has attracted a large number of industry insiders and outsiders, so that Dushan Jade is known, appreciated and accepted by more people.

Dushan jade is tough and dense, delicate and soft, transparent and mottled in color. There are 77 color types and 6 pigment types such as green, white, yellow, purple, red and black, which are the first-class raw materials for jade carving. Carving can be divided into decorative carving and plain carving according to different techniques. Decorative carving includes flower shaped censers, revolving censers, birds, animals, beautiful women and so on. Plain carving includes rings, bracelets, earrings and so on. Dushan jade carvings are glittering and exquisite. They are famous specialties of Nanyang.

After thousands of years of prosperity, the jade carving industry has formed a long-standing and profound Nanyang jade culture, which has bred generations after generations, handed down from generation to generation, emerged in endlessly, skilled Nanyang jade carving artists. While inheriting the traditional crafts, the masters of jade carving in Nanyang constantly introduce, absorb and innovate the techniques of art design and carving. It is precisely the combination of long history, profound cultural heritage and unique beautiful jade resources that makes Nanyang Jade Carving, an artistic treasure, develop and flourish.

第十一章　开封盘鼓

　　开封盘鼓又称"大鼓","中华五鼓"之一,是开封市特有的一种传统鼓乐表演艺术,也是河南传统民间文化活动的重要组成部分,在全国享有很高声誉。该民俗有凝聚民心、维系团结、怡情悦性的教化作用。原河南省文化厅将 1991 年称为"开封盘鼓年"。1999 年,开封盘鼓参加了澳门回归祖国的庆典仪式和中华人民共和国成立 50 周年大庆活动。

　　开封盘鼓是一种以鼓乐为主的表演艺术,鼓队由十几人至几十人组成,所用乐器只有大镲、人鼓、马锣三种打击乐器。这种形式的乐队,起源于古代军队中使用的一种鼓乐——讶鼓。北宋熙宁年间,讶鼓开始与传统民间舞蹈相结合。由于这种表演形式很受人们的欢迎,很快就在民间广为流传。到了明代,开封几乎所有的传统民间舞蹈表演都由讶鼓伴奏,因此,"讶鼓"便成为广义的开封传统民间舞蹈的统称。明代以后,"讶鼓"一词在开封消失了,但无论是纯鼓乐形式的讶鼓,还是由讶鼓伴奏的民间舞蹈"舞讶鼓",直到今天,仍在开封民间盛行不衰,只不过今天被称作"开封盘鼓"。

　　开封盘鼓所用乐器以鼓为主,配以大镲、马锣等铜乐器。鼓队无固定编制,规模可大可小,一般按"鼓二镲一"的比例组合。开封盘鼓表演时,由多人组成规模大小不一的鼓队,鼓队成员有的击打挎在身前的大扁鼓,有的敲击大镲、马锣等乐器,在"令旗"的指挥下,以"原地演奏"

与"行进演奏"两种方式表演，一边演奏着各种复杂的鼓点，一边列队行进在节日的街头、广场。全体鼓手既是乐器的演奏者，又是挎着鼓的舞蹈表演者。

作为一种古老的传统民间艺术，开封盘鼓气势宏大、震撼人心，鼓点激越、复杂多变；表演热烈、粗犷、豪放，无论是在音乐性上还是在舞蹈性上都有极强的艺术表现力和感染力，常能赢得观众的阵阵喝彩。因此，开封盘鼓深受城乡人民群众的喜爱，久盛不衰。

Chapter 11
Kaifeng Pangu

Kaifeng Pangu, also known as "Dagu", one of "the Five Chinese Drums", is a unique traditional drum music performing art in Kaifeng City, and an important part of traditional folk cultural activities in Henan Province. It enjoys a high reputation throughout the country. This folk custom has the edification function of cohesing the people's hearts, maintaining unity and pleasure. Former Henan Provincial Department of Culture declared 1991 as "the Year of Kaifeng Pangu". In 1999, the Kaifeng Pangu participated in the celebration of Macao's return to the motherland and the celebration of the 50th anniversary of the founding of the People's Republic of China.

Kaifeng Pangu is a kind of performing art mainly featuring drum music. The drum team is composed of people ranging from a dozen to several dozen. Only three percussion instruments are used: Dacha, Rengu and Maluo. This form of band originated from a popular drum music in the ancient army— Yagu. During the period of Xining in Northern Song Dynasty, Yagu began to combine with traditional folk dance. Because of the popularity of this form of performance, it soon spread widely among the folk. By the Ming Dynasty, almost all the performances of traditional folk dances in Kaifeng were accompanied by Yagu. Therefore, "Yagu" became the general name of Kaifeng traditional folk dances in a broad sense. After the Ming Dynasty, the word "Yagu" disappeared in Kaifeng, but whether it was a pure form of Yagu music or a folk dance accompanied by Yagu, "dancing Yagu", it is still popular in the Kaifeng folk today, but today it is called "Kaifeng Pangu".

The instruments used in Kaifeng Pangu are mainly drums, accompanied by brass instruments such as Dacha and Maluo. Drum teams have no fixed establishment and can be large or small in scale. They are usually combined according to the proportion of "two drums, one Cha (cymbal)". During the performance of Kaifeng Pangu, drum teams of varying sizes are formed by numerous people. Some members beat the big flat drums in front of them, others beat the Dacha, Maluo and other instruments. Under the command of the "command flag", they perform in two ways: playing in situ and playing in march. They play various complex drum beats while marching in line in the streets and squares of the festival. All drummers are both performers of instruments and dancers carrying drums.

As an ancient traditional folk art, Kaifeng Pangu has great momentum, with exciting drum beats, is shocking, complex and changeable; the performance is warm, rough, bold, with a strong artistic expression and appeal in music or dance, frequently winning the audience's applause. Therefore, Kaifeng Pangu is deeply loved by the people in urban and rural areas, and lasts for a long time.

第十二章　灵宝皮影

　　豫西的皮影戏以灵宝的最古老，可以说是灵宝古城的传世之宝。灵宝的皮影戏也叫道情皮影戏，是以高雅的道情演唱和轻盈的皮影表演演绎戏曲内容的一种庭院艺术。道情皮影戏的唱腔分为官调（喜调）和梅调（哀调）两种，演奏和演唱是二位一体的。2006 年，灵宝道情皮影被批准为国家级非物质文化遗产保护项目。

　　据有关史料记载，灵宝道情皮影源于明而盛于清，已有四五百年的历史。起初，只是几个人拿着不同的乐器聚在村头路边一起演奏，后来加了一些说唱故事，再往后发展到用剪影来表现，这一过程颇具电影发展史的风格。

　　一张白幕撑起，背后两位表演者手持侧面形象的人物，或撑或提，使人物变化出各种动作，然后利用光学原理，将人物形象和动作投影于幕帘上，让正面的观众欣赏。而在幕帘的一旁，还有一组人员使用各种民族乐器吹拉弹唱，配合幕后人的动作或演出剧目的故事情节，使整个表演浑然一体。这就是闻名于世的灵宝道情皮影戏演出场景。

　　道情皮影是灵宝特有的一个剧种。除了上述所需要的表演和演奏外，主要特点就是其唱腔使用了豫西方言。这种唱腔附位于所表演的故事情节，最终形成了自己独特的艺术风格。

　　道情皮影的另一大特色是皮影道具。它将传统的剪纸艺术运用在剪造各类人物形象上，与传统剪纸艺术不同的是，道情皮影使用的材料不是纸，而是动物的皮革。皮影以驴皮和牛皮为多，其中黄牛皮制作的皮影质量最好。剪刻的皮影道具，本身也是一种艺术收藏品，其人物栩栩如生、色彩鲜明，极具保存价值。

随着时间的推移，灵宝道情皮影从起初的单一型演变为现代的复合型，即从乐器演奏艺术到剪刻皮革艺术，再到唱腔艺术等，成为一门复杂又独具特色的地方艺术。

Chapter 12
Lingbao Shadow Puppetry

Shadow puppetry in Lingbao is considered the oldest of Western Henan, which can be said to be the handed down treasure of the ancient city of Lingbao. Lingbao's shadow puppetry is also called Daoqing shadow puppetry. It is a kind of courtyard art that interprets the content of opera with elegant Daoqing singing and light shadow puppetry. The singing tone of Daoqing shadow puppetry is divided into two kinds: Guan Diao (also known as "Xi Diao", a bright and cheerful tone) and Mei Diao (also referred to as "Ai Diao", a melancholic and sad tone). Performing and singing are two-in-one. In 2006, Lingbao Daoqing shadow puppetry was approved as a National Intangible Cultural Heritage Protection Project.

According to the relevant historical records, Lingbao Daoqing shadow puppetry originated in the Ming Dynasty and flourished in the Qing Dynasty. It has a history of four or five hundred years. At first, several people gathered on the roadside of the village with different musical instruments and played together. Later, they added some stories of telling and singing. Then, it further developed to be presented with silhouettes. This process bears a resemblance to the style of film development history.

A white curtain is held up. Two performers behind the curtain hold the characters of the side image, or support or hold, so that the characters can change various actions. Then, using the optical principle, the image and action of character is projected on the curtain, so that the front audiences can appreciate it. On the other side of the curtain, a group of people use various national musical instruments to play, pull and sing, cooperate with the action of the people behind the scenes or the plot of the puppetry, so that the whole performance is integrated. This is the performance scene of world-famous Lingbao Daoqing shadow puppetry.

Daoqing Shadow Puppetry is a unique opera of Lingbao. In addition to the above required act and performances, the main feature is the use of Yuxi (Western Henan) dialect in its singing. This kind of singing attaches to the story plot of the performance, and finally forms its own unique artistic style.

The other characteristic of Daoqing shadow puppetry is its props. It uses the traditional paper-cutting art to cut all kinds of characters. Different from traditional paper-cutting art, the material of Daoqing shadow puppetry is not the paper, but animal leather. Donkey hide and cowhide are the most common types of shadow puppetry, and the quality of shadow puppetry made of cattle hide is the best. The shadow puppetry props are also a collection of art. Their characters are vivid and colorful, and have great preservation value.

With the passage of time, Lingbao Daoqing Shadow Puppetry has evolved from a single type at the beginning to a modern complex type, that is, from the art of playing musical instruments to the art of cutting leather, and then to the art of singing, which has become a complex and distinctive local art.

第十三章 豫西剪纸

　　豫西剪纸是指流传于河南省晋豫大峡谷以南，南阳盆地以北地区的传统民间剪纸艺术。剪纸艺术遍布河南全省，豫西是河南剪纸最为集中、成就最高的地区。豫西剪纸艺术在全国享有盛名，其中，灵宝和卢氏的剪纸被列入国家级非物质文化遗产代表性项目名录，陕州区的剪纸被列为省级非物质文化遗产代表性项目。

　　早期的镂空雕刻艺术为剪纸的形成奠定了一定的基础，在纸被发明前，其艺术载体为皮革、金银薄片和玉片。南北朝时期，真正的剪纸作品开始出现，但在这一时期，它还未被大规模地传播。在公元7—10世纪的隋唐时期，剪纸已进入寻常百姓家。在960—1279年（宋代），剪纸在官府的倡导下得到了蓬勃的发展。

　　豫西剪纸色彩丰富。本色剪纸、套色剪纸、染色剪纸，一应俱全。其中，当地有一种独特的染色工艺，不用毛笔上色，而是直接放到和好颜色的碗中"蘸色"，调染后的剪纸浓淡相宜、过渡自然，极具特色。

　　豫西剪纸种类繁多。每到春节，当地人就在屋顶上贴"顶棚花"，门上挂"吊笺"，窗上贴"窗花"，灯笼上贴"灯笼花"，影壁墙上贴"春牛"，炕上贴"墙围花"，厨房、灶间贴"灶头花"。在喜庆的日子，当地人也要贴"喜花"。老人过生日，亲朋好友还要送"寿诞花"等。

　　吉祥是豫西剪纸作品中最重要的主题。在这些作品中，吉祥几乎无处不在。如"门笺"谐音是"门钱"，春牛意喻"耕种和丰收"，葫芦代表"福禄"，石榴代表"多子多孙"，牡丹象征"吉祥富贵"，满屋满墙全套的墙围花寓意"富贵不断头"。

豫西剪纸的风格因人而异。总体来说，豫西剪纸风格质朴粗犷、雄浑大气。更难能可贵的是，它所反映的生产、生活方式及思想观念，是几千年来农耕文化的延续，凝聚了中国传统民俗文化的内涵和特征。

Chapter 13
Paper–Cutting in Western Henan

Western Henan paper-cuting refers to the traditional folk paper-cutting art spreading in the south of Jin-Yu Grand Canyon and the north of Nanyang Basin in Henan Province. Paper-cutting art spreads all over Henan Province, Western Henan is the most concentrated and successful area of paper-cutting in Henan Province. Western Henan paper-cutting art enjoys a great reputation throughout the country. Among them, Lingbao and Lushi's paper-cutting are listed as representative items of National Intangible Cultural Heritage Projects, and Shanzhou District's paper-cutting is listed as representative items of Provincial Intangible Cultural Heritage Projects.

The early hollow carving art laid a certain foundation for the formation of paper-cutting. Before paper was invented, the earliest carrier of cutting art was the leather, gold and silver sheets and jade pieces. During the Northern and Southern Dynasties, real paper-cutting works began to appear, but in this period, it had not been widely disseminated. In the Sui and Tang Dynasties (7th—10th centuries), paper-cutting had entered the homes of ordinary people. From the year of 960 to 1279 (Song Dynasty), paper-cutting was vigorously developed under the advocacy of the government.

Western Henan paper-cutting is rich in colour, such as paper-cutting with its own colour, color-matching paper-cutting and dyeing paper-cutting. Among them, there is a special local dyeing process, not using a brush to color, but dipping colors directly from the prepared pigment bowl, dyed paper-cutting are properly blended, with natural transitions, which is very distinctive.

There are many kinds of paper-cutting in Western Henan. Every Spring Festival, the local people stick "ceiling flowers" on the roof, hang "door papercuts" on the door, stick "window flowers" on the window, stick "lantern flowers" on the lantern, stick "spring cattle" on the shadow wall, stick "wall flowers" on the adobe kang (for sleeping), stick "kitchen flowers" in the kitchen and on the stove. On festive days, local people also paste "happy flowers". Old people celebrate their birthdays, relatives and friends also send "birthday flowers" and so on.

Auspiciousness is the most important theme in the paper-cutting works in Western Henan. In these works, auspiciousness is almost everywhere. For example, "door paper-cuts" is homophonic to "door money"; spring cattle means "cultivation and harvest"; gourd means "fortune and prosperity"; pomegranate means "fertility and numerous descendants"; peony symbolizes "auspiciousness and wealth"; houses and walls fully covered with wall flowers implies "enduring wealth and prosperity".

The style of paper-cutting in Western Henan varies from person to person. Generally speaking, it is simple, rough and majestic. What is more precious is that the production, life style and ideas reflected in it are the continuation of farming culture for thousands of years, which embodies the connotation and characteristics of Chinese traditional folk culture.

第十四章　浚县泥塑

　　浚县泥塑是河南浚县的传统泥塑艺术品，其产地集中在城关镇杨屯。浚县泥塑始于隋末，传承至今，拥有极强的生命活力。其原料采用黄泥胶，分为泥咕咕派、泥猴派和泥玩派三大流派。其题材广泛、内容丰富、造型粗犷憨厚。2006 年，泥咕咕被列入第一批国家级非物质文化遗产名录。

　　豫北浚县，古称黎阳，是历代兵家必争之地。相传隋末农民起义领袖李密率领瓦岗军在此与隋军大战，伤亡惨重，将士们捏了泥人、泥马来祭奠阵亡将士。后来，百姓都效仿捏泥人来寄托自己的哀思。时间一久，捏泥人成了浚县的传统，泥人的题材也不再局限于战争。捏来捏去，平平常常的泥巴变成了古朴典雅的艺术品。

　　浚县泥塑的泥料就地取材，先将黄胶泥和成泥巴，用木棍捶打数十遍，使其细柔如面团。工具是一根木棍，削成一头粗一头尖，用来雕画花纹、打眼通孔。浚县泥塑题材广泛，既有历史名人也有各种动物。泥人多系历史人物，如徐懋功、王伯当、秦琼、尉迟敬德、程咬金、罗成等。禽鸟有燕子、小鸡、凤凰，走兽有小马、小猪、小猴，水族有小鱼、蛤蟆、乌龟等。

　　浚县泥塑发展至今，已分化出各具特色的三大流派：以王蓝田为代表的泥咕咕派（王派）；以"泥猴张"张希和为代表的泥猴派（张派）；以宋学海、宋庆春为代表的泥玩派（宋派）。王派采用传统手法捏制的泥咕咕可发出"咕咕"的声音，其造型古朴活泼、色彩斑斓。张派是以捏制泥猴而出名。宋派善捏制吹可发声的泥人、泥马、十二生肖等。三大流派的作品都在国际上产生了影响。

在浚县众多民间泥塑艺人中，最有代表性的民间泥塑艺术家是张希和先生。他捏的泥猴无人能比，被人们尊称为"泥猴张"，联合国教科文组织授予他"一级民间工艺美术家"的光荣称号，他的作品被国内外许多著名博物馆收藏。

Chapter 14
Xun County Clay Sculpture

The clay sculpture of Xun County is a traditional clay sculpture art of Xun County, Henan Province. Its origin is concentrated in Yangtun, Chengguan Town. Clay Sculpture of Xun County began in the late Sui Dynasty, passed down to the present, has a strong vitality. The raw material is yellow clay. It can be divided into three distinct schools: mud Gugu (whistling figurines), mud monkey (playful monkey designs), mud pillar (decorative spheres). Its themes are diverse, content is rich and the shapes are rugged and honest. In 2006, mud Gugu was listed in the first batch of National Intangible Cultural Heritage List.

Xun County in the north of Henan Province, known as Liyang in ancient times, has always been a strategic battleground contested by military strategists throughout history. According to legend, Li Mi, the leader of the peasant uprising at the end of Sui Dynasty, led the Wagang Army to fight with the Sui forces here, suffering heavy casualties. The soldiers then molded clay figures and horses to commemorate the fallen comrades. Later, the people imitated this practice by molding clay figures to express their grief. Over time, the clay figurine making has become a tradition of Xun County, and the themes of clay figurine are no longer limited to war. Through kneading and shaping, the clay became simple and elegant works of art.

The mud of Xun County Clay Sculpture is sourced locally. First, the yellow clay is made into mud and beaten dozens of times with wooden sticks to make it as soft as dough. The tool is a stick, which is sharpened so that one end is thick and the other end is pointed. It is used for carving patterns and drilling holes. The clay sculptures in Xun County have a wide range of themes, including both historical figures and various animals. The clay figurines are mostly historical figures: Xu Maogong, Wang Bodang, Qin Qiong, Yuchi Jingde, Cheng Yaojin, Luo Cheng and so on. Birds have swallows, chicks, phoenixes. Beasts have ponies, pigs, monkeys. Aquariums have small fish, toads, turtles and so on.

Up to now, the clay sculptures in Xun County have differentiated into three schools with different characteristics: the mud Gugu represented by Wang Lantian (Wang School), the mud monkey represented by Zhang Xihe (Zhang School), and the mud pillar represented by Song Xuehai and Song Qingchun (Song School). The mud Gugu made by the Wang School with traditional methods can produce the sound of "coo coo", which is simple, lively and colorful. Zhang School is famous for making mud monkeys. Song School is skilled in fabricating clay figurines, clay horses and the twelve Chinese zodiac signs, which can make sounds. The works of the three major schools have exerted an international influence.

Among many folk clay sculpture artists in Xun County, the most representative one is Mr. Zhang Xihe. His mud monkeys are unparalleled. He is honored as "Mud-Monkey Zhang". UNESCO has awarded him the honorable title of "First-Level Folk Arts and Crafts Artist". His works are collected by many famous museums at home and abroad.

第十五章　西坪民歌

西坪民歌是河南省南阳市西峡县西坪镇的传统民歌。西坪镇位于豫西伏牛山腹地，处于河南、陕西、湖北交界处，独特的地理与生活环境造就了丰富的地方民歌。2007 年，西坪民歌被列入首批河南省省级非物质文化遗产名录；2008 年，又被列入第二批国家级非物质文化遗产名录。

西坪民歌起源于汉朝，盛行于唐代，近两千年来绵延不断，显示出强大的生命力。西坪民歌内容丰富、个性独特，具有独唱、二人唱、多人唱、齐唱等多种演唱形式，乐器伴奏有无均可，在中原地区不多见。西坪民歌的类型有山歌、劳动歌、爱情歌、生活歌、儿歌等，其中劳动歌、爱情歌、生活歌地方特色浓郁。西坪民歌唱腔以真嗓为主，男声激昂、高亢、质朴，女声柔美、酣畅、奔放。既能抒情，又能状物，还能叙事，灵活自如，便于流传。

西坪民歌歌手利用这些传统的民族民间艺术形式走村串户，唱生活、唱爱情、唱历史，传承历史与文化、科学与生活、劳动与经验，丰富人们的精神文化生活。树荫下、火炉边、庙会上等人们聚集的场合，西坪民歌爱好者都会大放歌喉，西坪民歌已成为西坪镇重大节日、传统节日和日常生活最主要的文化活动载体。在文化艺术形式丰富多彩的今天，西坪民歌在西坪镇乃至豫、鄂、陕三省交界区域百公里范围内仍有较强的影响力和吸引力。

西坪民歌一直保持着世代相传、众人参与的传承体系，是一门有极高价值的民间艺术。为让西坪民歌重放异彩，西峡县通过整理出书、录音、制光盘等手段，对它进行了抢救性的保护。西峡县设立了西坪民歌保护基金，对现存老民间歌手进行保护，通过组建西坪民歌演唱队、举办西坪民歌大赛等活动，培养西坪民歌传唱队伍，让更多的人了解西坪民歌、演唱西坪民歌，使西坪民歌飞出深山、走向世界。

Chapter 15
Xiping Folk Songs

Xiping folk songs are traditional folk songs in Xiping Town, Xixia County, Nanyang City, Henan Province. Xiping Town is located in the hinterland of Funiu Mountain in Western Henan Province. It is at the junction of Henan, Shaanxi and Hubei. Its unique geographical and living environment has created rich local folk songs. In 2007, Xiping folk songs were included in the first batch of Intangible Cultural Heritage List of Henan Province, and in 2008, they were listed in the second batch of National Intangible Cultural Heritage List.

Xiping folk songs originated in the Han Dynasty, and began to prevail in the Tang Dynasty. They have lasted for nearly two thousand years, showing strong vitality. Xiping folk songs are rich in content and unique in personality, with many singing forms, such as solo singing, two-person singing, multi-person singing, chorus singing and so on. The accompaniment of musical instruments is optional and not common in Central Plains. The types of Xiping folk songs include mountain songs, labor songs, love songs, life songs and children's songs, among which labor songs, love songs and life songs have strong local characteristics. Xiping folk songs are mainly composed of true voice. The male voice is exciting, high-pitched and plain. The female voice is soft, smooth and unrestrained. It can express emotions, depict objects and narrate stories. It is flexible and easy to spread.

Xiping folk singers use these traditional folk art forms to go from village to village, singing about life, love and history. They inherit history and culture, science and life, labor and experience, and enrich people's spiritual and cultural life. When people gather under the shade of trees, by the fireside, at temple fairs and other occasions, Xiping folk songs fans will sing loudly. Xiping folk songs have become the primary carrier of cultural activities for major festivals, traditional holidays and daily life in Xiping. In today's rich and colorful cultural and artistic forms, Xiping folk songs still have a strong influence and appeal not only in Xiping Town, but also across a 100-kilometer radius in the border regions of Henan, Hubei and Shaanxi provinces.

The Xiping folk songs have maintained a system of inheritance from generation to generation, with the participation of all, which are a form of folk art with extremely high artistic value. In order to make Xiping folk songs shine through again, Xixia County has carried out rescue protection through means such as compiling books, recording audio, and producing CDs. Xixia County has set up Xiping Folk Songs Protection Fund to protect the existing old folk singers. Through the establishment of Xiping folk song performance teams and the organization of Xiping folk song competitions, Xixia County makes efforts to cultivate a new generation of Xiping folk song singers, so that more people can understand Xiping folk songs, sing Xiping folk songs, and make Xiping folk songs soar beyond the mountains and reach the world.

参考文献
References

[1] 白之仑.非物质文化遗产视野下的洛阳牡丹文化节——洛阳牡丹花会的当代流变研究［D］.北京：中国艺术研究院，2018.

[2] 拜珊珊.开封美食旅游开发研究［D］.开封：河南大学，2014.

[3] 汴平.文化菊城 别样芬芳［N］.开封日报，2015-10-18.

[4] 常兵.开封斗鸡［J］.中州今古，1995，2.

[5] 陈旭管.纪录片对非物质文化遗产的记录与书写［D］.福州：福建师范大学，2016.

[6] 陈彦丽.关于木版年画源头问题的探讨［J］.中国多媒体与网络教学学报（上旬刊），2018（9）：171-172.

[7] 褚净净.宝丰酒文化与文学书写［J］.科技展望，2016，26（28）：255，257.

[8] 董喆，李梦怡，胡越，等.信阳毛尖茶叶中矿物元素的主成分分析和品质评价［J］.食品安全质量检测学报，2019，10（1）：141-145.

［9］郭芳.灵宝道情皮影乐器艺术的传承与保护［J］.当代音乐，2016（7）：
　　50-51.

［10］郭杰，赵彦峰.复兴之路：千年汝窑的前世今生［N］.今日汝州，
　　2017-12-25（3）.

［11］郭良正.洛阳水席［J］.中国地名，2016（3）.

［12］郭师绪.品山品水品毛尖 信阳茶艺纵古今［J］.新产经，2018（6）.

［13］郝辉辉，顾军.洛阳南石山唐三彩烧制技艺传承研究［J］.自然与文
　　化遗产研究，2017（3）：134-138.

［14］郝娜，王亦兵.端午节的文化意义［J］.文学教育（上），2018（7）：
　　142.

［15］洪晓婷.冬至说"冬节"［N］.中国社会科学报，2018-12-25.

［16］黄浩."二月二"传统节日研究［D］.武汉：中南民族大学，2010.

［17］黄雅惠.再观豫剧《灞陵桥》——体味地方戏曲的传承与创新［J］.
　　中国民族博览，2018（12）：131-132.

［18］焦晨霞.豫西剪纸艺术的题材与意趣［J］.美与时代：美学（下），
　　2005（12）：59-61.

［19］孔静.河南浚县泥塑艺术的审美价值研究［D］.郑州：郑州大学，
　　2011.

［20］兰玲.冬至大如年［J］.走向世界，2017，52.

［21］兰玲.腊八节［J］.走向世界，2018（4）.

［22］李兰祥.纤云弄巧时 鹊桥相会日——七夕节与冯箕《七夕怀远图》
　　　［J］.老年教育（书画艺术），2018（8）：30-31.

［23］李鉴踪.略谈春节文化的精神内涵［J］.文史杂志，2019（2）：50-53.

［24］李珊珊.河南灵宝道情皮影研究［R］.开封：河南大学黄河文明与可
　　　持续发展研究中心专题资料汇编，2012.

［25］李晓红.灵宝道情皮影艺术初探［J］.兰州教育学院学报，2011，27
　　　（6）：32-33.

［26］李朝晖.节庆活动对城市文化建设的作用研究——以第32届中国洛
　　　阳牡丹文化节为例［J］.中共郑州市委党校学报，2015，135（3）：
　　　97-101.

［27］廉菊花，刘增学，熊维征.焦作市四大怀药特色农业发展研究［D］.
　　　郑州：河南工业大学，2016.

［28］梁艳，窦项东.南阳玉雕图案纹饰寓意研究［D］.西安：陕西师范大
　　　学，2013.

［29］梁卫红.刻画朴实传经典 文武门神迎新年——开封继中朱仙镇木版年
　　　画社藏品选粹［J］.东方收藏，2018，2.

［30］刘长乐，汤喜梅，崔军磊.新郑大枣矿质元素研究［J］.安徽农业科
　　　学，2008，36（24）：10419，10438.

［31］刘晨影，戴维娜.浅析开封盘鼓的庆典礼仪［J］.艺术研究：哈尔滨
　　　师范大学艺术学院学报，2015（4）：22-23.

［32］刘少鹏.试论少林武术文化的渊源与发展［J］.文教资料，2016（33）：
　　　68-69.

［33］柳莹.河南方言与地域文化［J］.鸡西大学学报：综合版，2011（10）：
　　　125-126.

［34］卢松.宝丰酒，开创清香回归的白酒新时代［J］.农村·农业·农民，
　　　2011（8）：45.

［35］卢旭.谈端午节的文化精神［J］.辽宁师专学报：社会科学版，2018
　　　（4）：40-43.

［36］卢刚.一个村，一部太极拳史［J］.农村·农业·农民，2018（6）：
　　　55-57.

［37］吕传彬.腊八节和腊八粥［J］.档案时空，2018（1）：38-39.

［38］吕红艳."二月二"节俗流变考析［J］.哈尔滨学院学报，2006（5）：
　　　70-73.

［39］马静.论浚县泥塑的艺术特征［J］.大众文艺，2010（15）：34.

［40］马全和.中秋节和"月文化"［N］.山西日报，2018-09-21.

［41］祁文文，袁率.开封盘鼓的文化传承与发展研究［J］.体育文化遗产
　　　论文集，2014.

［42］钱国宏.极富特色的元宵节活动［N］.中国文物报，2019-02-19.

［43］乔蓓芸，乔晓芸.拳种的研究——以陈式太极拳为例［J］.武术研究，
　　　2016，1（6）：31-33，39.

[44] 秦旪丰. 泥巴地里的曲艺盛会——马街书会 [J]. 照相机，2017（5）：8-11.

[45] 容本镇. 除夕 [J]. 南方国土资源，2019（1）.

[46] 尚晓丹. 河南南阳地区民歌现状研究——以西峡县丹江号子、西坪民歌为例 [D]. 武汉：华中师范大学，2018.

[47] 史友宽. 少林武术生命力的历史形成与未来发展 [J]. 南京体育学院学报，2018（6）：76-80.

[48] 宋国平. 中国曲艺的魅力——以河南省宝丰县马街书会为例 [J]. 大众文艺，2018（16）：140-141.

[49] 孙辉. 河南豫剧发展现状与展望 [J]. 北方音乐，2019（1）：95-96.

[50] 孙西玉，潘春梅. 张弓酒典型风格及其成因研究 [J]. 酿酒科技，2006（9）：94-95.

[51] 孙耀军，孙莉. 浅谈洛阳水席的起源与特色 [J]. 南宁职业技术学院学报，2011（3）：14-18.

[52] 王明磊. 非遗信阳毛尖制作技术传承与茶文化传播 [J]. 福建茶叶，2018，40（4）：371-372.

[53] 王佳. 南阳玉雕产业及玉料资源市场探究 [J]. 合作经济与科技，2016（5）：28-29.

[54] 王璞. 豫剧起源文化背景探析 [J]. 戏剧文学，2011（8）：37-41.

[55] 王翔. 河南道口烧鸡 [J]. 肉类工业，2013（11）：56.

［56］王晓峰.祭灶节有哪些习俗？［J］.文史天地，2019（2）：93.

［57］王晓峰.重阳节插茱萸［J］.文史天地，2019（2）：93.

［58］王晓峰.腊八节煮腊八粥［J］.文史天地，2019（2）：92.

［59］王晓俊，张露馨."一带一路"背景下豫剧文化的译介与传播路径研究［J］.新闻爱好者，2019（1）：58-62.

［60］王昕昱.浚县泥塑与泥猴张［J］.中国老区建设，2007（1）：51-52.

［61］王艺蒙.城市美食——河南名吃道口"义兴张"烧鸡［J］.美与时代（城市），2016（5）：92-93.

［62］王依农.那些不为人知的汝窑瓷器［J］.文物天地，2018（8）：76-85.

［63］吴京翰.叶县烩面 炝锅味道最留恋［J］.资源导刊，2015（3）：62.

［64］吴烨，田宜龙，逯彦萃，等.灵宝苹果香飘远［J］.发明与创新（大科技），2017（7）：18-19.

［65］夏莹.春节新民俗［J］.光彩，2019（3）：65.

［66］小雨.张弓酒鉴评会在郑州举行［J］.酿酒科技，2007（9）：97.

［67］徐春燕.豫西剪纸的历史发展与地域分布［N］.中国社会科学报，2011-09-22.

［68］闫林林.关于洛阳唐三彩历史展现的研究［J］.中国民族博览，2017（8）：99-100.

［69］杨靖.自媒体视域下西坪民歌保护初探［J］.黄河之声，2015（23）：104.

［70］杨梅.淮阳地区太昊陵庙会文化研究［D］.哈尔滨：黑龙江大学，2018.

［71］杨秋意，高阳.灵宝苹果，品质来自高度［J］.农村·农业·农民（A版），2017（4）：30.

［72］尧麟."年"的故事［J］.早期教育（家教版），2019（1）：42–53.

［73］姚腊华.汴绣遗产的文化价值评估［D］.开封：河南大学，2015.

［74］叶树良.道口烧鸡加工工艺研究［J］.肉类工业，2013（4）：12–13.

［75］于力申.论中原庙会文化及其现代意义——以淮阳太昊陵庙会为例［J］.佳木斯职业学院学报，2014（10）：36.

［76］张春雷.论南阳玉雕艺术对中国画的景仰和重构［J］.南阳师范学院学报，2015，14（11）：42–45.

［77］张冬霞.豫西剪纸的艺术特色及开发利用［J］.艺术研究，2015（2）：238–240.

［78］张浩，王强山.汝窑的发展及工艺特征［J］.现代装饰（理论），2016（8）：107.

［79］张舰戈.宋代中秋节日内涵演变考［J］.西南科技大学学报（哲学社会科学版），2018，35（6）：39–44.

［80］张舰戈.南北朝至唐代中元节内涵演变考［J］.唐都学刊，2019，35（1）：16–19.

［81］张舰戈.北宋中元节民俗活动内涵演变考［J］.南都学坛，2018，38（2）：20–23.

［82］张建萍.浅谈豫剧发展存在的问题及对策［J］.雪莲，2015（12）：
　　　61–62.

［83］张利宾.菊花文化节与开封城市形象构建和传播研究［D］.开封：河
　　　南大学，2014.

［84］张敏.变与不变——河南开封汴绣的传承与发展探究［J］.美与时代
　　　（城市），2017（4）：97–98.

［85］张文泉.九九重阳节 浓浓敬老情［J］.党的生活（黑龙江），2019（1）：44.

［86］张新刚，王媛，韩文生，等.焦作市怀山药气候适宜性种植区划研究
　　　［J］.安徽农业科学，2014，42（32）：11446–11448.

［87］张媛媛.蒸蒸日上话包子——品味开封［J］.农民科技培训，2015，
　　　8：45.

［88］张姚.中秋节——中国人的收割节与感恩节［J］.天风，2018（10）：
　　　38–39.

［89］赵华阳.浅析洛阳园林景观中牡丹文化的特征及应用［J］.现代园艺，
　　　2019（2）：120–121.

［90］赵军.西坪民歌初探［J］.东方艺术，2010：22–25.

［91］赵逵夫.同妇女及青年男女生活有关的七夕节俗［J］.西北民族大学
　　　学报（哲学社会科学版），2018，6：1–7.

［92］赵喜珠.太昊陵祭典庙会的特点及开发价值［J］.学理论，2015（3）：
　　　123–124.

［93］郑学富.古人如何过元宵节［N］.团结报，2019-02-14.

［94］卓卫华，张文杰，杨玲.河南新郑红枣以品质行走天下［J］.中国林业产业，2008（7）：63.

［95］周国平，李素荣.武陟油茶［J］.中州统战，1998（8）：43.

［96］周磊.开封斗鸡民俗现象及其社会意义［D］.开封：河南大学，2008.

［97］朱志平.从节气到节日："清明"节日化的时间及其历史逻辑［J］.南京农业大学学报（社会科学版），2018（5）：146-153.